YOUR RIGHTS WHEN STOPPED BY POLICE

SUPREME COURT DECISIONS IN POETRY AND PROSE

Nancy E. Albert, J.D.

**YOUR RIGHTS WHEN
STOPPED BY POLICE
Supreme Court Decisions in
Poetry and Prose**

Copyright © 2016 by Nancy E. Albert

All rights reserved. No part of this book may be used or reproduced by any means, graphic, electronic, or mechanical, including photocopying, recording, taping or by any information storage retrieval system without the written permission of the publisher except in the case of brief quotations embodied in critical articles and reviews.

LegalEase Press books may be ordered through booksellers.

LegalEase Press ISBN-13: 978-0-9971020-0-0

Printed in the United States of America

To the memory of my late Professor, Norval Morris,
who sparked my interest in working to improve the
American criminal justice system, and to my mentor,
Marshall J. Hartman, for his game-changing advocacy
on behalf of equal justice under the law.

Publisher's Note

This book offers general information on decisions of the United States Supreme Court relating to police-citizen interactions and Constitutional mandates. It does not purport to apply to the case of any particular individual or specific problem. The reader, therefore, should not assume that the information provided in this book is relevant to his or her situation. The author does not undertake to provide representation to any person through the use of this book. Many factors need to be weighed, such as state and local laws and state court decisions, before a given course of action can be recommended to an individual. Accordingly, if the reader has any doubts about proceeding on the basis of his or her own judgment, it is advisable to consult with an attorney. In addition, there is no guarantee that all of the information contained in this book will remain applicable after publication. There may be changes in the laws and in the interpretation of the laws by the courts. Any inadvertent errors that may appear in the text in spite of careful scrutiny are regretted by the author; however, there is no express or implied guarantee that the material is free from error.

CONTENTS

Preface	viii
The Constitution and Criminal Justice	1
Chapter One / Freedom of Speech and Breaching the Peace	2
Preaching: A Clear and Present Danger?	3
Fighting Words	5
Can You Cuss at a Cop?	7
How to Talk to a Cop	9
Marching, Singing, and Breaching the Peace	11
Chapter Two / Perspectives on Privacy	13
Your Home Is Your Castle	14
Sanctuary for Overnight Guests	15
Tainted Evidence Tossed Out	17
Phone Booths and the Fourth Amendment	21
Stop-and-Frisk	23
Tips and Traffic Stops	27
When Can a Cop Make a Traffic Stop?	30
A Stop on a Pretext	32
Search-Incident-to-Arrest	33
Searching a Traffic Offender	35
Curbing Car Searches	37
Rules of the Road	40
Is DNA Collection Orwellian?	43
The B-Guys: Can Refusing Testing Be a Crime?	46
Drivers to Exit on Command	49
Divulging Your Name	50
Stop and Identify	51
Not Free to Leave	53
Fuss on a Bus	55
Sobriety Checkpoints	57
Drug Detection Checkpoints	59
Can Anonymous Tips Provide Probable Cause?	60

A Chinese Puzzle	63
Cost-Benefit Versus the Constitution	66
Rights in Remission	69
Pooch on the Porch	72
Snooping with Sensors	74
Court to Big Brother: About GPS	76
Privacy in a Digital Age: Cell Phone Searches	79
When Is a K-9's Sniff up to Snuff?	81
A Sniff Too Late	83
Consent-Searches	85
Passengers Park Their Rights at the Curb	88
Rousting the Riders	90
An Exit for Passengers	92
Passenger Pat-Downs	94
Searches Limited by Time and Space	96
It Takes Two to Tango	98
Risky Roommates	100
Home Safety Inspections	103

Chapter Three / Turning the Tables 105

Can You Sue a Cop?	106
A Modality for Suing a Locality	107
Immunity and Impunity	108
Clearly Established Law	110
Deadly Force	112
Excessive Force	114
Driving While Black	116
A High-Speed Chase	118
Imminent Danger	121
Busted over Seatbelts	124
Till Sext Do We Part	127
Strip Searches in School?	131
Strip Searches in Minor Offenses	133
What It Takes to Win	136

Chapter Four / Representation, Self-Incrimination, and Identification 139

Gideon's Gamble	140
Lawyers Keep Out	143
D.A.s to Keep Mum about Silence	146
Miranda	147
Speak up to Remain Silent	150
Not So Mum Anymore	153
Miranda for Kids	157
Gideon Redux	159
Are Lawyers for the Poor up to Par?	161
Horse Trading	164
Vonlee and Her Guilty Plea	167
Should We Second-Guess an Eyewitness?	169
Chapter Five / Taking Aim at Gun Laws	171
Guns and the Constitution	172
Guns for Everyone	176
Guns and Domestic Violence	178
Don't Lie for the Other Guy	180
Chapter Six / Crime and Punishment	181
Juries and Liberty	182
Death Is Different	184
A Crime by Any Other Name	186
Juries and Mandatory Minimums	188
Punishing the Dealers	191
Insanity and the Death Penalty	193
Retardation and Execution	195
Too Young to Die?	197
A Fatal Number	198
Some Parting Words	200
Notes and Holdings	203
Table of Cases	250
About the Author	254

Preface

These verses tell the stories of real people and their run-ins with police and the criminal justice system. Their adventures, whether offbeat, comical, serious or tragic, most often culminated in arrest and prosecution. The stories revolve around this central question: after interacting with the criminal justice system, will the person prevail or end up in jail? A few of the sagas involve situations where citizens turned the tables by suing police for alleged misconduct.

The travails recounted here all landed in the United States Supreme Court for resolution. The nine Supreme Court Justices reached their judgments about who won and who lost by applying the framework adopted by Congress in 1791 -- the Bill of Rights.

Taken together, these Supreme Court decisions provide a road map to understanding the constraints imposed on the conduct of citizens and law enforcement officers alike. I hope that this book will leave the reader not only entertained, but also empowered by a better understanding of one's rights and responsibilities under the law.

Narrative poetry is used as a means of distilling the Court's opinions. For the sake of rhyming, I have employed a certain amount of poetic license. Accordingly, statements enclosed in quotation marks convey the gist of the ideas expressed, but do not necessarily contain the actual language used in the opinions. No offense to the Court or to the individuals whose travails are embedded in the nation's constitutional history is intended.

The name, date and legal citation for each case are provided in the Notes at the back of the book, along with its holding, written in prose. As used in the Supreme Court's written opinions, the words Court, Justices, and Members are capitalized when they refer to the United States Supreme Court.

While this book strives for accuracy, the Court's opinions are subject to differing interpretations. Some readers may wish to refer to the official court reports in order to draw their own conclusions. In addition to bound volumes of opinions such as the United States Reports and the Supreme Court Reporter, the full text of Supreme Court opinions can be found online at the Findlaw website,http://www.findlaw.com/casecode/supreme.html

One caveat may be helpful for those who are unfamiliar with the operations of our highest court. Since, barring exceptional circumstances, nine Justices sit on the Court, it takes only five Justices to constitute a majority. The majority view determines the "holding," that is, the decision, announced in each court case. If some Members disagree with the majority's decision, they may issue one or more dissenting opinions. Dissenting opinions help to illuminate the Justices' reasoning. Moreover, over time, the majority on the Court may shift by becoming more liberal or more conservative. The shift may ultimately lead to a dissenting opinion's becoming the majority view for a future Court. Consequently, some dissenting opinions are included in these poems.

THE CONSTITUTION AND CRIMINAL JUSTICE

The Framers, in seventeen ninety-one,
Said, "Now that our freedom has been won,
We'll lay down some safeguards to keep us free,
And protect our people for eternity."
They adopted ten precepts, the Bill of Rights,
To serve as our country's guiding lights,
And tacked them onto the Constitution,
To forge, for our nation, a lasting solution.
Here are some of the rules they sought to make plain
That, for criminal justice, are most germane:
In the First, they said, you may speak your piece.
(Even when in the presence of police!)
The Second says people may keep a gun,
When it's needed for defending everyone.
The Fourth is meant to protect you and me
With respect to one's person and property.
Amendment Five serves up a guarantee
Silence won't deprive us of liberty.
The Sixth gives the right to a trial and jury,
With counsel to stand up for equity.
And the Eighth says punishments shouldn't be cruel
Or unusual. (It's been an evolving rule.)
Then in eighteen hundred and sixty-six,
Congress said, "There's something we need to fix."
They added amendment number Fourteen
To make sure no unfair State laws would be seen.
These rules form the prism we use to refine,
For criminal justice, where we draw the line.

Chapter I. Freedom of Speech and Breaching the Peace

First Amendment: Congress shall make no law respecting an establishment of religion, or prohibiting the free exercise thereof; or abridging the freedom of speech, or of the press; or the right of the people peaceably to assemble, and to petition the Government for a redress of grievances.

Fourteenth Amendment: ... No State shall make or enforce any law which shall abridge the privileges or immunities of citizens of the United States, nor shall any State deprive any person of life, liberty, or property, without due process of law; nor deny to any person within its jurisdiction the equal protection of the laws.

Preaching: A Clear and Present Danger?

Jesse Cantwell got himself into a stew
For doing what Jehovah's Witnesses do.
He thought he was preaching the right and the good
In a Roman Catholic neighborhood.
He carried some books that bore a surprise --
The secrets for going to paradise.
His message included a second layer --
Records he played on a small record player.

He stopped two men on a city street corner.
They said they would hear what he had to offer.
"Enemies" was the name of a record he played --
Did he think that was how hearts and minds could be swayed?
It attacked the religion of the two men,
Who hoped never to hear such aspersions again.
It had not occurred to young Jesse Cantwell
That this type of language would never sit well
With those who adhered to their Catholic upbringing
And resented the record's gratuitous zinging.
Upon hearing the words in the record he chose,
They were sorely tempted to punch him in the nose.

The cops arrived, and Cantwell got arrested
For breaching the peace in a way some detested.
His message had an annoying proclivity
To foster anti-social negativity.
But did his lack of sensitivity
Reach the level of criminality?

Does the Fourteenth Amendment forbid the arrest
Of a person whose views many people detest?
The Supreme Court agreed to review the state's laws
To see if they complied with the Due Process Clause.

Said the Court, "We would never have the temerity
To condone what threatens the public tranquility.

But the charge against Cantwell was too general,
And religious freedom is too fundamental.
While stating one's views may lead some to anger,
Unless there's a clear and present danger
Of a threat to public safety and order,
We can't give police that kind of power.
His arrest abridges freedom of speech --
A state cannot forbid the right to preach."[1]

Fighting Words

If *Cantwell* spouted a grating repertoire,
Walt Chaplinsky's rant bordered on the bizarre.
He tried to draw followers to his flock,
Yet his expletives only served to shock.

Walt's actions seemed lawful and fairly correct
When he passed out pamphlets describing his sect.
But crowds grew restive at the very outset
When he slammed religion as a crooked racket.
The crowd soon began to push and to shove --
For Chaplinsky, they clearly showed no love.

Cops tried to contain them, without success,
So they put an end to the sorry mess.
When the top cop told him to end his gig,
Walt called him a crook and goddamned Fascist pig.
For breaching the peace, Walt got convicted.
Was the law, as written, too un-restricted?

New Hampshire's law seemed fairly comprehensive --
It forbad folks from using words plainly offensive
On any street or in a public place
Spoken directly to another's face.

While sticks and stones may shatter one's bones,
Can names wreak havoc like missiles and drones?
Did it breach Fourteenth Amendment Due Process
To ban a derisive mode of address?
New Hampshire courts vetted the law twice before.
With this case, it got to be tested once more.

Said the state court, "The public, by common consent,
Is well aware when 'fighting words' are meant.
Such words are intended to incite,
And ultimately lead to a fight.
The term 'offensive' is understood
By everyone in the neighborhood.

"Our law is plain and clear as can be --
It's all about using profanity
That's apt to provoke disorderly
Conduct among the community.
It's not too broad, but narrow and tight --
Our fighting words law is just about right."

On review, the Nine could not get excited
About the furor this case had ignited.
In a decision of nine-to-none,
The Court agreed that the state had won,
Since "fighting words" lead to injury,
Not order or morality.

"Epithets," said the Court, "Are not communication,
Since they fail to impart any real information.
The New Hampshire court has already construed
This law, so there's no more for us to conclude.
They've given it a narrow interpretation,
So we won't interfere with that situation.
Why should we be the ones to make a fuss?
What the state court held makes sense to us."[2]

Can You Cuss at a Cop?

Did a "Big Easy" ordinance overreach
By appearing to violate freedom of speech?
The law said when cops are on the job,
Whether you're alone or part of a mob,
You're not allowed to cuss, revile or swear
At the cops. You'll get pinched right then and there.

Like a Mama Bear out to protect her young,
Mallie Lewis was willing to risk getting stung.
If it meant that she could protect her son,
She would do whatever had to be done.
So she and her husband trailed a cop car
Where cops held their boy. They had not gone far
When a second patrol car forced them to stop.
After which, Mallie wound up dissing the cop.

The very first words the officer said
To Mr. Lewis when he exited,
Were: "Where's your g-- d-- license? Get up on your feet.
I'll teach you not to follow police down the street."
Said Mallie, "Sir, I want to know about my son."
But the cop replied, "Get back in your truck, woman.
Get your black ass back in the g-- d-- truck,
Or I'll show you something." Mallie felt dumbstruck.
Then she directed this expletive to the cop:
"You g-- d-- m-- f-- cops. This abuse has to stop."

The cop placed Mallie under arrest
For engaging the cop in a swearing contest.
In court, the judge found she broke the law,
Since her expletives were all he saw.
But she argued that the law was defective --
It swept too broadly, banning *all* invective.
The state courts disagreed, so this Mom and Pop
Pursued their complaint all the way to the top.

The Justices looked at how the law read,
And considered what the Court had said
When it held that *Chaplinsky* could be convicted
Based on what the "fighting words" law interdicted.
"But *this* law," they held, "is too broad on its face,
And we can't condone it in this type of case.
Words expressing a citizen's frustration
Need not provoke a violent confrontation.
It would be unlawful, unjust and absurd
To forbid folks from using a fighting word
When they're talking to cops, not to a crowd --
They've a right to express their thoughts out loud.
This law is too apt to lead to abuse,
Since cops could arrest folks with no excuse."[3]

How to Talk to a Cop

Did your mother ever say to you,
"Speak only when you're spoken to?"
Is that admonition over the top
When the one you're talking to is a cop?

The City of Houston passed a law
That seemed to contain a serious flaw.
The city enacted a total ban
On words or acts by a woman or man
That interrupt, even quietly,
A cop engaged in the line of duty.

A honcho of Houston's Gay Political Caucus
Ran afoul of the law for being too raucous.
Raymond Hill emitted a shout of protest
When a handicapped man was placed under arrest.
When Hill, in the aftermath, got arrested,
He saw a chance for the law to be tested.
His goal -- to garner a bit of immunity
From harassment aimed at the gay community.

So Hill came to court loaded for bear.
He brought in a big stack of cases where
Folks got arrested for cursing or talking,
Or refusing to move instead of just walking.
In one case, a person decided to linger
Long enough to give a policeman the finger.

Hill's case went to the High Court in due time,
And the Court constructed this paradigm:
"This type of law is not narrowly tailored --
It gives the police too much unfettered
Discretion to harass folks and condemn
Anyone who doesn't agree with them.
When 'fighting words' are addressed to police,
They're less likely to cause a breach of the peace,
Since police who have been properly trained

Are surely expected to act more restrained
Than a person that you've never met
Who'd likely react to an epithet.

"Amendment One means you can speak your piece,
Even when you're talking to the police.
It means folks may criticize and challenge
Cops while seeking to convey their message.
Where a law lacks curbs to keep cops in their place,
Such a law is invalid on its face.
Plastic surgery can't help it to survive,
So we vote to kill it, not keep it alive."

Several Jurists chimed in, "While we agree
That the Houston law should be history,
If someone attempts to deliberately
Keep a cop from performing effectively,
That may be banned by a municipality
With a law that is drafted more skillfully."[4]

Marching, Singing, and Breaching the Peace

Abraham Lincoln freed the slaves,
But rights for their progeny came in waves.
The Fourteenth Amendment sought to guarantee
Essential human rights and dignity.
Congress hoped it would lead to tranquility.
In the South, it failed to achieve equality.
Former slaves felt a sense of futility,
And wondered if it held any utility.

In the sixties, a breath of freedom blew in
To liberate the grandkids and kin
Of those who had to take a back seat
When they sat on the bus or at a place to eat.
A group of new leaders tried to advocate
That it was high time to desegregate.

In nineteen hundred and sixty-one,
For a group of students, the campaign had begun.
In a South Carolina church where they met,
They spoke quietly and posed no threat.
Their goal -- to protest discrimination
With marching and determination.

They walked 'round the State House in an orderly way,
And displayed their signs to have their say.
Then they heard a speech, and in a patriotic manner
The group joined in singing "The Star-Spangled Banner."
They wanted lawmakers to heed their plight --
They hadn't come there to pick a fight.

At first, the cops said, "Sure, you can come in."
But when onlookers gathered, their patience grew thin.
Cops saw, sprinkled in the gathering crowd,
Troublemakers growing boisterous and loud.
Authorities feared that without intervention
There'd soon be a surge of spontaneous combustion.

Cops told the group's leader, "You must disperse,
Or things could become decidedly worse."

When cops told the group to get off the street,
The youths started clapping and stamping their feet.
So while nearly two hundred students protested,
The City Manager had them all arrested.
But the simmering crowd who had gathered en masse --
All three hundred of them ended up with a pass.
The students got charged with "breaching the peace" --
That's what it was called by the local police.
But state courts provided the admonition
That the term never had an exact definition.

Said the Court, "May an offense be criminalized
If the acts it entails are so generalized?
Free speech is annoying and provoking --
The fires of prejudice it may be stoking.
But First Amendment rights cannot be invaded.
In the Fourteenth Amendment they're incorporated.
This standardless law is too open-ended.
It has no constraints that should be defended.
The students' convictions cannot stand
In America, this promised land."[5]

Chapter II. Perspectives on Privacy

Fourth Amendment: The right of the people to be secure in their persons, houses, papers, and effects, against unreasonable searches and seizures, shall not be violated, and no Warrants shall issue, but upon probable cause, supported by Oath or affirmation, and particularly describing the place to be searched, and the persons or things to be seized.

Fourteenth Amendment: ... No State shall make or enforce any law which shall abridge the privileges or immunities of citizens of the United States, nor shall any State deprive any person of life, liberty, or property, without due process of law; nor deny to any person within its jurisdiction the equal protection of the laws.

Your Home is Your Castle

Let's take a good look at Amendment Four,
Which stops cops in their tracks at your front door.
It tells us that we have a right to be free
To count on our homes for security,
And that warrants are needed to barge right in.
When cops fail to get one, they cannot win.
If cops witness a crime in the public square,
They can make an arrest right then and there.
But unless a judge has found probable cause
To believe that you've broken any laws,
The cops must not enter to make an arrest
Without passing a magistrate's stringent test.
Though your home might be frail, and might shake and sway,
Its walls give you the power to have it your way.[1]

Sanctuary for Overnight Guests

On Saturday morning, some bad stuff went down
At an Amoco station in the heart of town.
A lone gunman. A robbery. Shots rang out.
The clerk was dead, without the slightest doubt.
Cops thought they knew who had done the deed,
And drove to his home with all due speed.
They managed to find the getaway car
Near the shooter's home -- It hadn't gone far.
They nabbed the shooter, though he'd run away,
But the driver escaped, to the cops' dismay.
The abandoned car, on the other hand,
Contained lots of info and contraband.
A car title showed Rob Olson's name,
So cops figured he's the one to blame.

On Sunday, someone called cops to say
She knew who drove for the getaway.
She gave them the address where he'd gone to stay,
And said Olson was leaving town that same day.

Cops checked out the address, a two-unit place,
Where the grandmom lived in the first floor space.
She confirmed that her granddaughter's gentleman friend
Had been staying upstairs -- a terrific Godsend!
She promised to give the cops a heads-up
The minute she saw Rob Olson show up.

The lead cop had a practice he wouldn't mend --
He never sought warrants on a week-end.
Instead, he issued an arrest bulletin,
Ordering local cops to take Olson in.

It didn't take long -- an hour or two
Before cops heard back, and moved into view.
They dashed up the stairs, lest Olson be gone,
Then broke into the unit, with their guns drawn.
They found him in a closet, cringing in fear,

And arrested him once they saw their way clear.
The 19-year-old told them he'd thought they'd stopped
At the station to buy cigarettes and pop,
Till the shooter returned with a bag and gun.
Then he feared the shooter and wanted to run.

The case reached the highest court in the land,
Where the Jurists endeavored to understand
What the Founders meant by the right to be free
In our "homes," persons, papers, and property.
Should the Fourth Amendment, when put to the test,
Protect privacy for an overnight guest?

"The cops could have obtained a warrant," they said,
"Then the matter would quickly be put to bed.
But given the facts, did Olson's arrest
Satisfy the Fourth Amendment's test?
Overnight stays are deemed an amenity
Recognized as useful by society.
Houseguests have a right to expect privacy
Without intrusions on their security.
Therefore, Olson's warrantless arrest
Violated the Fourth Amendment's test."[2]

Tainted Evidence Tossed Out

In the sixties, the Court set out to reform
Police behavior falling short of the norm.
About half the state courts had declined to crack down
On warrantless raids in a city or town.

To the Court, the Bill of Rights was sacred,
But without state compliance, its mandates were naked.
So how could the High Court impose its will
And make the states take such a bitter pill
When most folks believed the Constitution creates
Two distinct spheres of government -- federal and states?

Federal courts already followed the rule
That tainted proof gets tossed out as a tool
For convicting a suspect who without it
Would get discharged and cease to be a target.

Well, around 1960, a case came along
Where the hapless defendant had done nothing wrong.
Dollree Mapp and her daughter lived in a home
With a roomer who suddenly opted to roam.
He left behind stuff that was old and worn,
Including some items of rather soft porn.
Once Dollree learned he did not plan to stay,
She packed up his things while he was away.
Then she moved the items out of her sight,
So he could retrieve them whenever he might.

Before his return, three cops came to her door.
She hadn't a clue what they'd come there for.
She phoned her lawyer, and he was clear
That she had nothing at all to fear,
For without a warrant, the cops had to stay out.
So she went to the window and gave them a shout,
Saying, "You've no right to enter my place,
Nor a right to begin searching this space."

But the cops, who'd received a bum tip from some tipster
Could not be convinced to take no for an answer.
They firmly believed that a fire-bombing louse
Was hiding out somewhere inside Dollree's house.
The cops hung around, surveilling the dwelling,
And several hours later, their numbers were swelling.
Seven cops swarmed the home, and one broke her door.
Then some charged upstairs to the second floor.

Her lawyer showed up, but cops kept him from entering,
And she couldn't hear a word he was uttering.
Cops slapped her in handcuffs and twisted her arm --
They seemed intent upon doing her harm.
Though they peered in each cupboard and searched each drawer,
They never found who or what they came looking for.
They rummaged for leaflets about bomb-making,
But no such leaflets were there for the taking.

Then despite the trauma that Ms. Mapp had borne,
She got charged with a crime -- possession of porn.
When asked for a search warrant, the D.A. came up short.
Should the porn have been approved for use inside the court?
The jury found her guilty, since the charge rang true.
When told she'd have to go to jail, she knew not what to do.

On appeal, counsel argued the Fourteenth Amendment
Prohibits a seizure without a search warrant --
"Due Process" means that fairness is needed,
And Dollree's case showed it was not heeded.

Ohio's courts had no prior decision
Banning tainted proof from a prosecution.
While conceding the case seemed to smack of unfairness,

Their courts concluded that Ms. Mapp had no redress.

The Supreme Court saw a sea change unfolding,
And agreed to review a prior holding
That the Fourteenth Amendment's Due Process guarantee
Doesn't make a state court into a referee
Who throws the gains from an unlawful play
Out of the game and makes them go away.

The Justices said, "There's a growing movement
Among state courts to share in the judgment
That unlawful seizures leading to a conviction
Should not be rewarded by the shield of court sanction.
An 'Exclusionary Rule' is a harsh means to compliance,
But all milder reforms have been met with defiance.

"We cannot stand by while a state lets a cop
Invade people's privacy; that has to stop.
It's time to close the last courtroom door
Left open for proof rotten at its core.
We reject the claim that the Fourth Amendment ban
On unreasonable search and seizure can
Only apply to the federal sphere.
States must grant Due Process. This is now clear:
The Fourteenth Amendment incorporates the Fourth,
And the states must adhere to its dictates henceforth.
Before, U.S. courts and state courts across the street
Followed different rules -- now, the two have to meet.

"So we hold that state courts must now refuse
To use proof gained through lawlessness and ruse.
When the cops break the law,
They can't use what they saw.
All evidence that's ill-begotten
Is going to have to be forgotten.

"If the cops become lawbreakers, they breed contempt
For the law; thus, no state or town should be exempt.

The Rule of Exclusion's an excellent way
To curb abuses when police go astray."
Dollree's nightmare would last no longer,
And the Bill of Rights became much stronger.[3]

Phone Booths and the Fourth Amendment

There once was a time before smart phones, forsooth,
When people placed calls from a telephone booth,
And tools for surveilling were not like today's --
The Feds did their work in more low-tech ways.

This story dates back to nineteen sixty-five.
The Feds had a hunch, but needed to strive
To compile enough info for probable cause
To believe that a suspect was breaking the laws.

Charlie Katz was a bookie, or so they believed.
When they dreamed up a plan, they felt very relieved.
They saw him use pay phones on a daily basis,
And decided to bug his pay phone oasis.
They stuck bugs on top of the phone booths with tape,
And with a tape recorder, their plan took shape.

For seven days, they recorded his betting,
And after that time, Feds knew they were getting
Some evidence to use when he took the fall
For betting by making an interstate call.

But at trial, the defense said, "Hey, wait a minute --
The Fourth Amendment says there's a limit
On searches and seizures by Government --
You can't bug a phone booth without a warrant.
Thus, the tapes from the bugging cannot be used
To convict Mr. Katz; his rights were abused."

The State disagreed. The A.G. said:
"There's no violation on the part of the Fed.
There was no intrusion into Katz's space,
Since the bugs were on the outside of the place.
The phone booth was never penetrated,
So use of the tapes should be vindicated.
He cannot complain of the intruding eye --
A glass phone booth invites a bystander to spy."

When the case reached the highest court in the land,
The Jurists declared: "Cops must understand:
We do not adhere to the narrow view
That property interests provide the clue
To determining when a person's rights
Are invaded by an electronic device.
It need not be a physical thing
To be deemed worthy of protecting.

"When Katz entered the booth, what he sought to exclude
Were not eyes, but meddling ears that intrude.
It's not a question of what one can see --
In a booth, we're right to expect privacy.

"Tell cops who want to stay in our good graces,
The Fourth Amendment shields *people*, not *places*.
So prior to bugging the calls of a suspect,
Cops must get a warrant; that's what we direct."[4]

Stop-and-Frisk

Justice Warren penned this case in '68,
And from day one it stirred a great debate.
It grew out of something rather innocuous --
A mundane thing that could happen to all of us.

Two men stood in wait on a downtown street,
Until joined by a third they'd planned to meet.
A detective picked up on that simple sight,
And sensed there was something that didn't look right.
When asked to explain it, he couldn't say why --
His years on the streets made them catch his eye.

Patrolling in plain clothes, he noticed the men
Strolling past the same store again and again.
He guessed they were casing an upscale shop,
And suspected there'd soon be a stick-'em-up.

The cop asked the men for identification,
But got only mumbling and no information.
Then he grabbed the three men, spun them around,
Held them together, and patted them down.
He felt their coat pockets, and two men were packing.
Did it matter that grounds for arrest were lacking?

Terry's journey had only just begun
When he took a fall due to his hidden gun.
He and his bud were in a dreadful funk,
Since the case against them looked like a slam dunk.

In court, counsel argued, "The cops break the laws
When they make an arrest *sans* probable cause
To believe that the suspect committed a crime
Or is fixing to do so within a short time.
After all, the cop saw them commit no sin,
As store windows are meant for looking in.
Thus, the guns the cop seized when he made the arrest
Should not be admitted; they must be suppressed."

The trial judge went out on a legal limb,
Though his odds of avoiding reversal looked slim.
Some believed the trial judge took a pretty big risk
When he held, "That was no *arrest*, just a 'stop-and-frisk.'
The stop was for the officer's protection,
Lest matters should turn in a tragic direction."

Then came a hue and cry from the defense bar
That this new-fangled rule went a bridge too far.
Should the need of cops for self-protection
Condone a fishing expedition?

The High Court agreed to hear the argument
That admitting the guns breached the Fourth Amendment.
"To be sure," said the Court, "It's a novel conclusion
That an afternoon stroll may draw a cop's intrusion.
Until now, this Court has avoided its mention
Lest 'stop-and-frisk' lead to community tension.
Did it breach Terry's right to security
To be stopped and frisked for walking in the city?
This delicate aspect of police activity
Is one we must handle with great sensitivity.

"A brief 'stop-and-frisk' is not an arrest,
So it isn't required to meet the same test.
When a cop keeps a person from walking away,
He does 'seize' the person who then has to stay,
And a public pat-down is no small indignity --
It's a serious slap at a person's sanctity.

"While it's one thing to bolster police security,
It's another to bestow admissibility
On the fruits of a search without probable cause
To believe that the suspect is breaking the laws.
The rule excluding tainted proceeds from a case
Has the goal of deterring rogue cops at its base.

YOUR RIGHTS WHEN STOPPED BY POLICE — Nancy E. Albert

With no sanction, the Fourth Amendment guarantee
Against improper searches would be quite empty.

"Still -- criminals, in their quest for booty
Kill many cops in the line of duty.
We can't deny those who serve and protect
The chance to counter a likely threat.

"If a reasonable cop finds the conduct suspicious,
Then a stop, if it's brief, is not too pernicious.
But a stop can't be based on a simple hunch --
Any cop who thinks that is out to lunch.
The cop's rationale must be quite specific,
Else a stop-and-frisk would be too horrific.
A pat-down must stem from reasonable suspicion
That the target is involved in the commission
Of a crime a 'prudent man' would deduce
Is bound to involve a weapon's use.

"And one more thing -- cops must limit their intrusion
To outerwear pat-downs to check for a weapon.
The new rule we announce protects a cop
By allowing guns seized in a *Terry*-type stop
To be used as proof in a criminal case,
Where the stop was justified in the first place.
We now put folks on notice to be wary
Of a stop-and-frisk authorized by *Terry*."

Justice Douglas figuratively shook his head,
Since the ruling confounded him. Then he said:
"This rule gives the cops unjustified power
To seize someone simply due to his glower.
The term 'probable cause' rings a bell of certainty
Embedded in our Constitutional history.
But 'reasonable suspicion' sounds too technical,
And prudent rules call for something more factual.
In adopting this policy we're sealing our fate
By turning into a totalitarian State.
This case is a blot on our institution,

Since it's clearly at odds with the Constitution.
Every citizen will need to be wary --
No one is secure in the wake of *Terry*."[5]

Tips and Traffic Stops

Decades after *Terry* made its debut,
Cops still struggled to find a clear-cut clue
As to what the decision allowed them to do.
Might it lead to police work that some would eschew?

An event on a highway of scenic beauty
Left the courts debating, "Did cops do their duty
When they stopped a truck based on a telephone tip
That the driver veered over the median strip?"

One afternoon, from Highway One,
A female caller dialed 9-1-1.
She reported a truck that suddenly showed
Up and forced her to drive right off of the road.
Her anonymous tip came out of the blue.
Were cops right to believe her story was true?
She gave them the pick-up's plate number and make
To assist them in any action they'd take.
But can it be deemed "reasonable suspicion"
When cops use a tip without verification?
Were cops right to believe that they had enough?
Might the call have been a mean-spirited bluff?

The cops found the truck driving along the shore,
And followed it for five minutes or more
To see whether the truck moved recklessly,
But the driver handled it carefully.
Cops forced the truck to stop on the shoulder,
Then left their squad cars and ambled over.
As they neared the pick-up's parking spot,
The highway patrolmen plainly smelled pot.

When the case came to court, defense counsel said,
"Police in this instance were quite misguided,
Since they had no grounds for reasonable suspicion
To believe there was a traffic violation."
But the state's courts insisted they were very

Sure cops had a right to stop based on *Terry*.

Was the 9-1-1 call too unreliable
To render the traffic stop justifiable?
The Supreme Court agreed to grant review
To decide if *Terry* would allow this stop, too.
The Jurists locked horns, voting five-to-four,
Saying, "We wish these cops had a little more --
This looks like a remarkably close case,
But the cops are often caught in a race
To prevent drunk drivers from causing great harm,
So the tip sufficed to sound the alarm.
We give her points for accuracy --
It enhances her credibility,
And the fact that she saw it with her own eyes
Lowers the odds that the call was a guise.

"There's one more reason why we'll let a cop
Make an unverified traffic stop:
 9-1-1 comes with technology
That provides lots of specificity.
Phony callers seeking retribution
Would wind up facing swift prosecution."

Justice Scalia wrote a lengthy dissent,
Lambasting the majority's argument.
"A 9-1-1 call can't support a stop
Without proof that could guide the highway cop.
Where one swerve is reported to 9-1-1,
What does that prove to anyone?
Anonymous tips must be corroborated
Before assuming a law was violated.
Indicia of the tip's reliability
Are needed to give it credibility.

"While callers cannot remain unknown,
That proves nothing unless it is shown
That the tipster knew she could be caught
For making a phony traffic report.

The majority leaves out one pesky detail --
Cops observed that the driver never did fail
To follow the law as he drove for five
Minutes whilst they tracked him along the drive.
A driver soused enough to swerve
Can't control his car around a curve.
Therefore, this flimsy, unverified tip
Provides no excuse to let our rights slip.
The majority's freedom-destroying cocktail
Will risk having our freedom of movement curtailed."[6]

When Can a Cop Make a Traffic Stop?

One evening in nineteen seventy-six,
A Delaware cop trolling out in the sticks
Decided to waylay a car driving by,
Though he couldn't come up with a good reason why.
Then as passengers exited from the side door,
He spied pot in plain view right on the car floor.

The driver got charged in criminal court
With pot possession. But his stay was short.
His lawyer managed to get him off the hook
By showing the cop hadn't played by the book,
Since the cop admitted on the witness stand
He had nary a clue they had stuff that was banned.
Nor had he witnessed a traffic violation,
Or anything giving him grounds for suspicion,
Until *after* he'd waylaid the car in question.
That must have given the D.A. indigestion.

The trial judge was not being facetious
When he called the stop wholly capricious.
He said such a stop is impermissible,
So the evidence seized is inadmissible,
Then promptly ordered completely dismissed
The charge against the aggrieved motorist.

But once the D.A. regained his composure,
He sought to give the Diamond State closure.
He said random checks for license and registration
Would help to make roadways safer in our nation.
He argued that cops should not be constrained
When they seek to have drivers briefly detained.

The case made its way to our highest court.
The Justices' answer was clear and short:
"Cops have no right to decide at their leisure
To make an unjustified search or seizure.
The goal of the Fourth Amendment's proscription

Is to guard against unbridled discretion.
Folks are not shorn of that basic protection
When they venture outdoors at their election.
If the cop has observed no violation,
He can't make a stop to check registration.
Cops are obliged to stick with the tradition
Of making stops only with grounds for suspicion,
And the grounds must be based upon a good reason,
Since on drivers, we've declared no open season.
We view checkpoint stops in a different light,
Since such stops are less apt to engender fright.
But we hold random spot checks to be a no-no,
So suspicionless stops will remain a no-go."[7]

A Stop on a Pretext

Two vice-squad cops were spending time
In a neighborhood known to be high-crime,
When they drove past a truck stopped at a light.
They could see the black occupants, though it was night.
The cops didn't see them do anything wrong,
But sensed the truck idled a little too long.
When the cops circled back to investigate,
They reached the truck just a few seconds too late.
It made a quick turn and sped off to its right,
Neglecting to flip on a turn-signal light.
The cops chased down the truck and pulled up alongside
To see if the young men had some secrets to hide.
Sure enough, when one cop sauntered up from the back,
He saw a guy holding two large bags of crack.

Should a minor technical violation
Serve as the basis for incrimination?
A mere pretext was all it was
When the driver's truck was stopped by the fuzz.
Where the police lack probable cause
To believe that a driver broke any drug laws
Before stopping his truck and making an arrest,
Should the drugs they observed therefore be suppressed?

In court, the cops said all they were planning
Was to give the driver a simple warning.
Counsel argued that cops are obliged to hold back
From stopping drivers due to driving while black.
Since there are so many traffic laws,
Cops could target folks without much cause.
Do pretextual stops pose an inherent danger
That can foment and foster community anger?

A unanimous High Court weighed in,
Holding the cops had committed no sin.
As long as they saw traffic laws being broken,
They could stop the truck, though for reasons unspoken.[8]

Search-Incident-to-Arrest

Ted Chimel concocted a plan quite chimerical --
Some called it bizarre, or even hysterical.
This scheming, shortsighted petty crook
Figured the owners would overlook
His theft of rare coins because they were insured,
So that small inconvenience would somehow get cured.
In chats with the owners, he threw out the pitch
That insurance fraud could make them rich.
The garrulous Chimel had also made mention
To one of his buddies about his intention.
When the break-ins occurred, owners thought they knew
How they happened, and spoke to some men in blue.

Three cops arrived late in the afternoon.
Chimel's wife told them they'd come too soon
If they were hoping to see her spouse --
He was still at work, and not in the house.
They sweet-talked her into letting them in
While they waited for their chat to begin.
The cops kept their secret close to the vest --
They were armed with a warrant for his arrest.
When Chimel came home, a big, burly cop
Nabbed him for the hoist of a rare coin shop.
They asked for permission to look around,
Since they planned to seize any proof they found.
Chimel objected, but they had a hunch,
And told him the law allowed them *carte blanche*.
The officers searched the whole house for an hour,
Thinking the arrest warrant gave them that power.
They grabbed enough coins and such to think
It would land Ted Chimel in the clink.

The Nine agreed to accept the case
To deal with a question that courts have to face:
What factors should define the test
For conducting a search-incident-to-arrest
Where the search wasn't authorized by a court.

Did the warrantless search by the cops fall short?

Said the Court, "We've allowed a narrow exception
To the Fourth Amendment's basic conception
Requiring a search warrant that specifies
Precisely what items a search may comprise.
When a valid arrest is executed,
The simple fact can't be refuted
That police have ample justification
For a limited search at that location.
The inherent needs of the situation
Call for some sort of accommodation.

"But should cops be given a license to zoom
In and search one's garage and every room
Without obtaining judicial approval
Before scooping up items for removal?
In the absence of some grave emergency,
We're obliged to protect people's privacy.
So here are the limits that we must impose:
Incident-to-arrest, cops may search the clothes
Of the suspect to make sure there's no way he
Could endanger the officer's own safety,
And may seize things within his direct control,
Even stuff that might land him in the hole.
But the search is required to stay within
Reaching distance of the space he is in.
Searching other rooms to see what's hidden
From now on will be strictly forbidden."[9]

Searching a Traffic Offender

Willie Robinson got caught in the debate
Over whether police should have to wait
And seek a search warrant after an arrest.
His case put that question to a test.

A cop saw him driving a Caddy in D.C.,
And said to his partner, "That guy lied to me.
I checked out his permit, and say what you will,
It's as phony as a two-dollar bill."
So they stopped Willie's car in that D.C. hood,
And told him, "Your driver's permit's no good.
You're under arrest for 'operating after revocation
And obtaining a permit by misrepresentation'."

In accord with D.C. police procedure,
The cops decided it was not premature
To commence a search of Willie's coat,
Where they found contraband worthy of note.
They drew from his pocket a cigarette pack,
And found it contained capsules full of smack.

So Willie got caught with drugs in his pocket,
But after his case was placed on the docket,
Counsel said, "Though cops made a lawful arrest,
The drugs that they found have to be suppressed.
Where the bust is just for a traffic violation,
The scope of a search requires modification."

Said the cops, "It's not like a *Terry* stop on 'mere suspicion.'
We had 'probable cause' to believe his commission
Of a criminal act, although traffic-related.
So to *Terry*'s restrictions, we're not subjugated.
Terry's rules should be limited to brief stops,
Not to full-fledged arrests effected by cops."
The trial court allowed the drugs to come in,
And ruled that he possessed heroin.

The Appeals Court had a different take --
"The trial court failed to give him a break.
Although for a drug crime Willie was tried,
The search for drugs could not be justified.
There could be no proof of a traffic crime
In a search of his person at that point in time.
This search violates the Fourth Amendment,
And so we reverse the trial court's judgment."

The Supremes, by a vote of six to three,
Said, "We are inclined to disagree.
Where the search is 'incident to a lawful arrest,'
An exception to the warrant requirement is best.
This search complied with all the laws,
Since the arrest was based upon probable cause."

Three Justices, in dissent, said, "Whoa!
This isn't the Fourth Amendment we know,
Where a neutral magistrate is asked to decide
When a cop is allowed to peer inside
The clothes of one found behind the wheel
While simply driving an automobile.
In a traffic stop, cops may feel for a gun,
But that's only allowed for their protection.
Just 'cause a police department has a rule
Doesn't give cops the right to use it as a tool
To search outside the lines of a Constitution
For which we fought the Brits in a revolution."[10]

YOUR RIGHTS WHEN STOPPED BY POLICE — Nancy E. Albert

Curbing Car Searches

The tip cops received was strictly anonymous,
So they tried to act cool and not raise a big fuss.
They strode up to the door with an air carefree,
And asked, "Are you the owner? Or who might you be?"
The guy at the door was named Rodney Gant.
He said, "I'd love to chat, but right now I just can't.
If you come back later, you can meet the owner;
He'll be back in the house shortly before supper."

Cops left and did their homework, since their standards were demanding.
Gant's license was suspended, and a warrant was outstanding.
They returned to the house soon after dark,
And found a couple with their car in park.
They arrested the male for giving a false name,
And found drugs on the female in the same time frame.
Cops cuffed them and sat them in the squad car,
And before cops had time to say "*Bonsoir*,"
Gant's car drove up, and they saw it was him,
Despite the fact that the light had grown dim.

Gant parked in the driveway, and proceeded up the walk.
He was yards from his car when cops swooped down like a hawk.
Without so much as a "How do you do,"
Cops slapped on the cuffs, and when they were through,
One more squad car arrived, and they locked him inside it.
They found coke in his car -- he had no way to hide it.

At Gant's drug trial, the defense lawyer contended,
Once they had Gant cuffed, their authority ended
To search Gant's car without his consent,
Since the law required them to get a warrant.
Said the trial court, "Police could search Gant's car, since
He was under arrest for a traffic offense,

And cops may search incident to arrest.
That's settled law there's no way to contest."

Civil rights groups claimed, "It invades one's privacy
To give cops such unfettered authority.
What harm could an officer possibly fear
If the suspect is cuffed and his car's not near?
This drill puts a dent in American freedom;
It's a practice we need to put the brakes on."

Gant won his case in the state's highest court,
But the case went up to the court of last resort.
For Gant to win there might take a miracle --
He was up against a daunting obstacle:
A rather old case did not point in his favor,
So Court-watchers wondered if Jurists would waver.
That case from the eighties appeared to attest
Cops may search a car incident-to-arrest.

Said the Court, "We're keenly aware there's a chorus
Of judges and scholars all asking for us
To revisit our precedent's clarity.
Does it pay Amendment Four fidelity?
For twenty-eight years, academies have taught cops
They have an entitlement in traffic stops.
Those guilty of a simple traffic violation
Have had their personal security taken.
Cops should not confuse a narrow exception
With the right to search at their own election.

"So now we would like to make one thing clear:
If a driver is cuffed and no longer near
His car at the time his arrest is effected,
Cops can't search the car. Our old case stands corrected.
We will, nonetheless, cut cops some slack --
There is one thing that we will take back:
If the bust wasn't for driving, and cops believe
There's proof of that crime, we'll give police leave
To go and search the passenger compartment,

And bring stuff they find to the police department.
But make no mistake, with respect to one's car,
The old search-incident-to-arrest rule went too far."[11]

YOUR RIGHTS WHEN STOPPED BY POLICE — Nancy E. Albert

Rules of the Road

It's a Rule of the Road that's not hard to follow --
The way to obey it is, mind what you swallow,
Since it's long been the law in every state:
Blood-alcohol must stay below point oh eight
For drivers who get behind the wheel,
No matter how sober they might feel.

Tyler McNeely, he let things slip. See,
He left a bar feeling rather tipsy.
At two a.m., the truck he drove was weaving,
Till a cop pulled him over and said, "You're speeding."
When he rolled down the window, it was easy to tell
By his bloodshot eyes, speech, and the alcohol smell
That he was impaired, so the cop asked this question:
"Just how much booze have you been ingestin'?"
"Just a beer or two." (His nose might have been growing.)
Said the cop, "So I guess you wouldn't mind blowing
Into this device. Then you won't have to stay;
If you pass, I'll be sending you on your way."

"I couldn't do that," McNeely demurred;
"I'm in a rush, so that must be deferred."
"Nice try," said the cop, "but now our next stop
Is a clinic nearby -- just a skip and a hop.
I need a blood sample, so I want your consent."
"Over my dead body. If you're hell bent
On taking my blood, I won't sit still.
You'll have to do it against my will."

Then the cop advised him, since it was that state's norm
To read the law from a preprinted form:
"Refusing the test is a wrong of the sort
That suspends your license and will be used in court."

"Okay, take my license if that's the game,
But I won't give permission all the same."

Well, the cop ignored McNeely's objection,
And took him to the clinic for blood collection.
Then a lab technician drew a sample.
It wasn't a lot, but yet was ample
For the sample to register point one five four,
Which was double the number McNeely'd hoped for.

So McNeely got charged with DUI,
And the cop told the court the count was too high.
Then McNeely piped up, "The blood draw was a search that
Required a search warrant. Put that in your high hat!"
Said the D.A., "Wrong! When it's alcohol-related,
Liquor in the bloodstream is so quickly dissipated
That *any* DUI should count as an emergency,
And the law allows exceptions in case of urgency."
"Not so!" said the judge. "Drunkenness is no crisis.
Such a blanket assumption is plainly amiss.
Cops might think there's *carte blanche* to get a blood draw,
But without a warrant, they're breaking the law."

The High Court agreed to consider this question:
Is a crisis created by a driver's digestion?
Said the Court, "Invasions of bodily integrity
Uproot long-held expectations of privacy.
The D.A. is right that we'll make an exception
Where an exigency points in that direction.
BAC ratios do dwindle with time,
But the numbers do not turn on a dime.
Cops can seek a warrant by phone or email.
If a judge can respond, then cops must not fail
To get a warrant for piercing a driver's skin,
As long as the process can be done within
The time frame that is needed to prevent
Loss of evidence when there's no consent.

"Will this weaken the laws against driving drunk,
And leave Mothers Against Drunk Driving in a funk?

Not at all, because there are other tools
To use against those who break the rules.
The D.A. may continue the prosecution
Based on proof that complies with the Constitution.
Drunk drivers may get their license revoked,
But without a warrant, they can't be poked.
Or, at the least, we're very emphatic --
A cop's right to poke is not automatic.
A cop needs to consider all the facts
Before, with a knee-jerk, he suddenly acts."[12]

Is DNA Collection Orwellian?

A man named Alonzo Jay King
Did a very frightening thing --
In a group of people, he grabbed a gun
And pointed his weapon at everyone.
No one got hurt, but King was arrested.
Then cops did something the man detested.

Without his permission, before he could speak,
They swabbed DNA from inside of his cheek.
The cops sent the swab away to be tested --
They did that for violent suspects arrested,
Since Maryland's law said there's no need to wait
Till a person's convicted in their state.

After waiting four months, the Lab got a hit --
King's swab matched DNA from an old rape kit.
Then the cheek swab led to a rape indictment.
King bristled, and cried out with great excitement:

"It breaches the Fourth Amendment," he protested.
"That wasn't the reason why I got arrested.
My swab was a 'search' without grounds for suspicion,
So state law is at odds with the Constitution."
But the trial judge decreed, "I see no such loophole;
You get life in prison with no chance of parole."

The Court of Appeals saw things differently:
"That law breaches the notion of privacy.
Cops may swab DNA from a *convicted* felon,
But *this* practice is banned by the Constitution."

The Supremes said, "Lower courts are conflicted --
Should DNA swabs be tightly restricted?
Should such testing ever be inflicted
On suspects arrested but not convicted?
We'll decide whether cops may pursue the mission
Of testing for crimes without grounds for suspicion.

"The issue need not cause us such paralysis.
The Fourth Amendment's not our sole analysis.
A cheek swab *is* a 'search;' this we do admit,
But that is not the long and short of it.
A search must be reasonable in scope and execution.
Does a swab meet that test? Now here's our conclusion:
Cops need to know who it is they are booking,
And a DNA test is one way of looking.
A suspect's criminal history
Is an integral part of his I.D.
DNA is a tool that's so effective,
It's better than hiring a skilled detective.

"It's not like the case where they pierce someone's skin,
Since to draw the guy's blood, they have to go in.
But a cotton swab is so soft and gentle,
It can't breach a right that is fundamental.
DNA is just like a fingerprint,
Yet it's better and more significant.
Defense attorneys can vent their spleen,
But booking with swabbing is just routine.
The invasion here is so minimal,
Opposing it is almost criminal.
There's no risk at all; the accused will be fine.
By golly, how could a test be more benign?
If a suspect is lawfully under arrest
For a serious crime, we think it is best
That a cheek swab be deemed a reasonable seizure
When it's part of a routine booking procedure."

Four Members of the Top Court's Nine,
In dissent exclaimed, "Hold the line --
Our system bans searches without grounds that point to guilt.
That's the basis on which the Fourth Amendment was built.
Research shows swabbing so soon is not problem-free --
One-third of us get arrested by age twenty-three.

"It's merely an optical illusion
That there is no physical intrusion.
When we invade a body cavity,
We can't pretend that it lacks gravity.
Comparing it to fingerprints bears scrutiny --
We've never ruled on their legitimacy.
But fingerprints are used for identification.
In contrast, DNA is for investigation
Of facts not involving the crime of arrest.
This suspicionless search fails the privacy test.

"The scope of this holding is vast and scary --
Innocent folks may become its quarry
When their data goes into a registry.
Who says that can't happen to thee and me?
How ironic -- those later acquitted of crime
Will have their DNA stored for all time.
Just how far will this novel doctrine go?
Will we start testing those who drive too slow?
Would the proud souls who wrote the charter of our liberty
Meekly open their mouths for checking by the powers that be?"[13]

The B-Guys: Can Refusing Testing Be a Crime?

Here's a true story about three guys
Whose driving habits were quite unwise.
Three close encounters happened when
The cops caught up with each of them.
Birchfield drove his car into a ditch.
A truck stuck in the drink became Bernard's glitch.
Beylund nearly clobbered a stop sign,
Since he couldn't navigate a straight line.
All three drivers reeked of alcohol
When cops paid the impaired men a call.
Blood tests or breath tests were demanded,
And driving permits, revoked or suspended.

A new law raised the bar in North Dakota,
Along with a new law in Minnesota.
They added the sanction for refusing a test
From just yanking a license to jail, post-arrest.
Birchfield and Bernard got sentenced to jail
For declining a test they were destined to fail.
Beylund complied, but appealed, complaining
That his test was "coerced" by the officer's warning
That refusing a blood test would be a crime
For which he could wind up doing hard time.

Once those new laws set out to raise the bar,
The Court pondered whether they'd gone too far.
Should refusing to take a warrantless test
For blood-alcohol lead to a driver's arrest,
With conviction for a separate crime
And the prospect of doing extra time?
Did it violate the Fourth Amendment
To require consent without a warrant?
The Court compared cases decided before
The B-guys' petitions wound up at their door,
Like *Tyler McNeely* and *Alonzo King*,
And decided to simplify everything.

YOUR RIGHTS WHEN STOPPED BY POLICE

Nancy E. Albert

"In the *King* case, we held it was O.K.
To swab someone's cheek for DNA,
Because a swab is so soft and gentle,
It can't breech a right that's fundamental.
Likewise, requiring a driver to blow
In a straw is fine, and not a no-go!
It's just like inflating a party balloon!
Why wait for a judge? It's never too soon!
The Fourth Amendment's not implicated
When breath tests are so regulated.

"But McNeely's case told us a warrant's required
To draw someone's blood, unless time has expired,
And refuseniks may get their license revoked,
But without a warrant, they can't be poked.
That's assuming cops have time to apply
Before too much time has already flown by,
Since booze in the body may dissipate
In about two hours; then, it's too late.

"So we've come up with a mixed decision,
And we now state it with great precision:
A warrant's required when cops want to go in
With a needle and puncture a person's skin,
But we hold that one's privacy's not invaded
By a breath test; it need not be debated!
Since a breath test itself is not abhorrent,
We rule that cops don't require a warrant."

Two dissenters said, "We do not agree --
We see forced breath tests quite differently.
Our colleagues decided to draw a line
Between blood and breath tests. But, by design,
The Constitution's requirements were meant
To apply unless facts are exigent,
Such as 'hot pursuit' when things look dire,
Or rushing in to put out a fire.

"Most motorists seem to be quite gullible --

They assume roadside tests are reliable.
That is a common misconception,
And leads to the motorist's deception.
A standard breath test is done at the station
With devices not prone to equivocation.
Roadside tests can't be used as evidence
In a court if suspects get a good defense.

"The need for speed, it can't be debated,
Is based on numbers that are inflated.
So when cops have time to fax or email
A judge, then cops should not ever fail
To seek a warrant before either test,
Whether blood or breath. Here's what, we suggest:
The warrant process won't add to the delay --
It's important to let judges have their say.
This hairsplitting is so clearly contrary
To the Fourth Amendment, it's arbitrary."[14]

Drivers to Exit on Command

When the cop pulled Mimms over for an expired plate,
The stop was legit, and that fact sealed his fate.
Though the cop had no grounds to suspect foul play,
He told Mimms to get out on that fateful day.
He said that's his drill -- it's a routine precaution
Each time he stops a car for a violation.

When Mimms stepped out, the cop noticed a bulge
That Mimms would have preferred not to divulge.
The cop patted him down, and lo and behold,
He found a gun. But there's more to be told.

The state's top court said the gun should be suppressed,
Since the Fourth Amendment had been transgressed.
When the cop ordered Mimms to exit the car,
That was an unconstitutional bridge too far.

But the U.S. Supremes said, "We do not agree.
Such a minor incursion on liberty
Is merely a petty indignity
That can't balance concerns for a cop's safety.
It's a reasonable invasion of a driver's security
That this Court already approved in *Terry*."

Three dissenters said, "This goes far beyond *Terry*.
We would have decided it to the contrary.
The cop had no grounds to suspect a crime,
Let alone that a gun would be found this time.
In Mimms' case, the cop had nary a clue
Before telling Mimms what he had to do.
This case expands *Terry*'s narrow tool,
And sets up a very broad new rule."[15]

Divulging Your Name

When meeting a cop, it's always been true --
You don't have to reply, "How do you do?"
But are you required to give your name?
The answer is not always the same.

A Texas man called Zachary Brown
Took a stroll in a dicey part of town.
When cops asked him to stop and state his name,
He declined and he began to complain.
A cop said to Brown, "You're under arrest
For failing to give your name and address,"
Since Texas law said that's what you must do
Anytime you're stopped by the men in blue.
Brown was required to pay a small fine,
'Cause his silence, by law, was out of line.

Brown filed an appeal, and he protested,
"I never should have been arrested.
This law violates the Constitution,
Since stopping folks is too great an intrusion
Where cops lack a reasonable suspicion
That a person is on a nefarious mission."

The Court looked at the facts, and unanimously
Said, "Under these circumstances, we agree --
The law breached Brown's right of privacy,
Since a cop could demand his identity.
The benefit seems to be small indeed,
Balanced against what the state law decreed.
Fourth Amendment guarantees do not allow it.
As for Brown's conviction, we hereby reverse it."[16]

Stop and Identify

How do you know, when you're walking along,
Humming a tune or singing a song,
And you see a cop, what's in his head --
Could you tell before any words are said?
What if he thinks you're involved in a crime --
How would you know that ahead of time?

Nevada had a "stop and identify" law
Like the Texas one where the Court found a flaw.
Nevada's law said a cop may detain
A person and ask him to give his name
If a cop has grounds for reasonable suspicion
That the target's involved in some crime commission.

When a cop first stopped Larry Hiibel,
Larry had no way to really tell
If the cop suspected him of a crime,
Or merely wanted to take up his time.
In fact, the cop had received a phone call
That a man with a truck was involved in a brawl.
The officer did not hesitate --
He sped to the scene to investigate.
It was clear that Larry had more than a few
Bottles of an extremely strong brew.
The cop said he was being investigated,
And Larry became angry and agitated.
When the cop asked him to show his I.D.,
Larry yelled, "Why not go and arrest me?"

When Hiibel got convicted, he brought up *Brown*.
He said Nevada's law, too, should be struck down.
The High Court replied, "Many states have these laws,
Much like *Terry* stops without probable cause.
Some are no good because they're so unclear,
They don't tell what info one must volunteer.
Texas law didn't call for reasonable suspicion
Before putting a guy in an awkward position.

But Nevada's statute is more precise --
To comply, you don't need to roll the dice.
A suspect need only reveal his name --
A *Terry* stop allows the same.
Like *Terry*, Nevada requires a belief
That a crime is involved, and the stop must be brief.
Asking questions is part of investigation,
And 'What's your name?' is not an interrogation.
One's name is an attribute that's universal.
It's not a big deal requiring reversal."

Four Justices out of the Top Court's Nine
Used the occasion to opine:
"Prior cases say cops may ask for I.D.,
But no answer's required by a detainee.
Terry suspects have always been free
To decline, since that goes with one's liberty.
It's a Fourth and Fifth Amendment right --
This case should be thought of in that light."[17]

Not Free to Leave

DEA agents stood silently,
Watching each passenger carefully,
As they exited the flight from L.A.,
Hoping to nab a courier that day.

They spotted Sylvia, the last to deplane.
Her appearance could best be described as mundane.
There was nothing specific to catch their attention
That one might consider worthy of mention.
Though they lacked any reasonable grounds for suspicion,
The agents proceeded to carry out their mission.

She walked very slowly across the airport,
And the DEA agents brought her up short.
"Can we see your I.D. and plane ticket?" they said.
She handed them over, nodding her head.
When they scanned both documents for her name,
They noticed the names were not the same.
They told her they were from the DEA,
And asked what if anything she had to say.
"I just felt like using that name," she replied,
As she stood there looking nervous and wide-eyed.
They handed her license and ticket back,
But agents sensed they were on the right track.

"Would you follow us? We need to talk,"
Said one agent. "Our office is just a short walk."
She gave no reply, but followed along,
Up a flight of stairs as they slipped through the throng.

What happened next, she hadn't anticipated.
The situation rapidly escalated.
They first asked to search her purse, and added,
"You've the right to decline," but she said, "Go ahead."
Her purse contained a ticket to L.A.,
In a third person's name. It was not her day.

A female cop showed up, seeking her okay
To search her person before she went away.
She was told to strip naked. There was no turning back.
She withdrew from her panties two baggies of smack.

In court, counsel argued that when the cop
First approached her and forced her to stop,
He had no good reason, simply put,
To think criminality was afoot.
The stop was a "seizure" *sans* adequate cause
To believe she was breaking any laws.
So the heroin found as a fruit of the seizure
Must be suppressed due to his misbehavior.
The trial judge held the stop was good under *Terry*,
And her cooperation was voluntary.
But the Court of Appeals strongly disagreed,
Saying, "Even if we were to concede
The initial stop had been permissible,
What followed was very reprehensible.
Taking her to the office at their behest
For questioning constituted an arrest.
Thus, consent to the search was not validly given.
The search was the fruit of a lawless detention."

Had the Fourth Amendment been violated?
That is the question the High Court debated.
Said the Court, "Sylvia could have walked away --
She'd no basis for thinking she had to stay.
The initial approach was not a seizure,
Since she could have ignored it at her leisure.
No matter the lack of any advisements
That she could decline to show her documents."

So after extensive deliberation,
The Court set in stone this new formulation:
"A person may only be thought of as 'seized'
If she reasonably thinks she is not free to leave.
She'll need to weigh all the circumstances
To assess the odds before taking her chances."[18]

Fuss on a Bus

The "war on drugs" has stirred up such a stew,
Cops must assess what they can and can't do.
At an airport, train station, or bus depot
They've had to explore just how far they can go.
Some sheriff's departments have made it their mission
To waylay travelers without grounds for suspicion.

Two Florida deputies boarded a bus.
They hoped that their presence would not raise a fuss.
Symbols of their power were clearly not lacking,
Such as badges and pouches showing they were packing.
They eyed the crowd, and without hesitation,
Asked one dude to show his identification.
There was nothing about his ticket or I.D.
That led them to start up a colloquy.
"We'd like to inspect your bags," they insisted.
Their probing query could not be resisted,
Since the dude, Mister Bostick, felt he must comply --
He could not walk away or just say goodbye.
He was stuck on a bus with nowhere to go,
And had to endure whatever would follow.

Well, the search of one bag turned up some coke,
And the officers said, "This is no joke,"
Since we're narcs, and it is our job to arrest
You, since finding drug dealers is our main quest."
When Bostick's case came to court for trial,
There was no point in offering a denial.
He argued that the court should censure
The narcs for making an unlawful seizure,
Since they lacked any basis to suspect
Him of crime, so their seizure was not correct,
And the coke they found ought to be suppressed.
That would finally put the case to rest.

Amendment Four said we should be secure
Against any unreasonable seizure.

How should the courts balance the right to be free
With protecting the public's security?
How much weight must we give to autonomy
And a person's inherent right to privacy?

The Court asked, "Should this type of police encounter
Always be deemed an unlawful seizure,
Since a law-abiding bus passenger
Can't simply walk away at his leisure?
Here's what we see as most fundamental:
The encounter has to be consensual.
Now it's true, Bostick claims he did not consent
To the search of his bag, but that's just argument,
Since the trial court found that was not how it went --
He allowed them to search the luggage compartment.
The narcs told him he had the right to refuse,
So he's bound by the choice that he opted to choose.
As long as their actions did not tell the story
That consent to their search was mandatory,
It's hard to see what harm is meant
By a little search when there's been consent.
We don't see these events as intimidation;
So this we conclude with no equivocation:
As long as consent is voluntary,
We won't decide to the contrary."

Three dissenters objected, "The answer is no.
That's not how this case was supposed to go.
Although we're involved in a war on drugs,
Cops don't have a right to behave like thugs.
Dragnets are fine for a show on TV,
But they're not okay for you and me.
The suspicionless sweep is like tyranny.
Under our law, that's not how it ought to be.
In Hitler's Berlin and Stalin's Moscow,
Human rights were the first thing to go."[19]

Sobriety Checkpoints

The State Police crafted a checkpoint plan
To stop and inspect every woman and man,
Looking for signs of intoxication,
Despite a dearth of grounds for suspicion.
The stop was designed to be brief and cursory,
So the stop, the cops thought, had little gravity.

They did a trial run in Saginaw County,
Where they tested two drivers for sobriety,
And sent scores of others on their way
After a twenty-five second delay.

Some drivers went to court to complain
That the State Police plan would be a pain,
And transgress the Fourth Amendment prohibition
On detaining folks without grounds for suspicion.
The trial and appeals courts said, "The drivers are right.
The old 'balancing test' makes their case airtight --
The stops surprise drivers and cause them fright,
But their effectiveness is very slight."

Then the U.S. Supremes voted six to three:
"When it comes to this class of minimally
Intrusive stops, the scale shifts the other way,
So sobriety checkpoints are here to stay.
They're nothing at all like a random stop
Made by a patrolling unconstrained cop.
The traveler's concern or fright is far less
When all drivers are stopped -- that is our guess.
The Fourth Amendment is not violated
Where the risk of drunk driving is obviated."

Dissenters said, "Such suspicionless seizures
Cause damage that cannot be measured.
These checkpoints are mostly conducted at night
In an unannounced spot, which makes folks uptight.
Valid suspicion is a core protection

Of the Fourth Amendment against State action.
Not only are such plans too audacious,
Results show they are not efficacious.
A mere two arrests out of 125
Hardly justifies keeping this program alive.
These checkpoints lack adequate justification.
We should keep our eyes on the Constitution."[20]

Drug Detection Checkpoints

Since the Court had not objected at all
To checkpoints screening for alcohol,
One city crafted a plan so sublime
For interdicting drug trafficking crime.
They set up roadblocks where no one could decline
Exterior sniffs by a well-trained K-9.

James and Joell each sought an injunction
Against cops stopping folks with no compunction
About the lack of grounds for suspicion
That they were involved in crime commission.
The cops said in reply, "Why make such a fuss --
For a five-minute stop, why go after us?"

So the Nine took up the issue again
About using checkpoints to halt crime when
The crime causes lots of social harm.
But the Court said, "This causes us great alarm.
It is not like a threat to life and limb,
Where loss of life could be very grim.
We're quite concerned when the program's goal
Is primarily about crime control.
The Fourth Amendment is intended to screen
This type of intrusion from being routine.
When it comes to roadblocks designed to fight crime,
That's where we've decided to draw the line."[21]

Can Anonymous Tips Provide Probable Cause?

When cops seek a search warrant, they need to swear
To an impartial judge that there is some there, there.
Their oath must be written, and should do no mincing
Of facts that are detailed and convincing.

Local cops got a letter from no one knew who --
It showed up at the station out of the blue.
It said that "A couple behaves like thugs,
Since they make their living by selling drugs.
Their name is Gates, and they live in your town.
On May third, Sue will drive their car down
To Florida, where she'll make a buy.
She'll leave the car there and then she'll fly
Back home while the car gets loaded with pot.
Then Lance will fly down and drive back with the lot.
What's more, there's a stash in their domicile
Of drugs that would make a police raid worthwhile."

The cops commenced to track the pair,
And learned when Lance took to the air.
Local cops got help from the DEA,
Who followed the two as they wended their way.
The couple's travels somewhat matched the route
That the snitch described when he ratted them out.
But they drove home together to Illinois,
So the snitch made a flub when predicting their ploy.

Based on the letter and secret surveilling,
Cops prepared an affidavit detailing
How use of a plane and the interstate highway
Fit the couple's alleged *modus operandi*.
They stapled the letter to their sworn statement,
And a magistrate issued a search warrant.

When the couple came home, they got a surprise --
Cops swarmed the place like a bunch of flies.
In their car, cops found bundles of marijuana,

And their house had more pot, plus drug paraphernalia.

But the trial judge found that cops broke the laws,
Since the letter did not provide probable cause
To believe the home of the pair named Gates
Contained contraband as the letter states.
Plus, the cops' independent investigations
Failed to confirm the note's accusations.
That corroboration, although well-meant,
Only showed conduct that looked innocent.

The state's highest court said, "We agree --
The affidavit lacked believability.
Anonymous tips are presumed unreliable,
So two things are needed to make them seem viable:
Some facts to show how the snitch came to know
All that supposedly damning info,
And some reason to trust the snitch's veracity,
Like a record of proven credibility."

But the U.S. High Court said, "For an unsigned letter,
We have a test that works much better.
Facts that tell how the snitch came to know all that stuff,
And that he wouldn't stage some ginormous bluff
Are nice, but we can't mandate every facet,
Lest we place the cops in a darned strait jacket.
In order to justify 'probable cause,'
You can't be so picky in looking for flaws.
As the term implies, it's about probability,
And cops shouldn't need to guarantee certainty.
Rigid rules don't belong where there's such diversity --
It's not like a course in a university.
It's the *totality of circumstances*
That, in the end, enhances the chances
Of a judge's decision to issue a warrant
Needed for use by law enforcement.
Affidavits are drafted in haste for investigation,
So one can't expect lots of specification.
We don't want to raise the standards so tall

That cops won't apply for warrants at all.
If the judge has substantial facts for concluding
That a search would uncover proof of wrongdoing,
We'll permit the judge to use common sense
Based on all the facts used as evidence."

The dissenters said, "No; this new rule has a flaw --
Its litmus test is a major change in the law.
Now warrants may issue when some unknown snitch
For some unknown reason pitches a bitch.
This snitch never told how he reached his conclusion.
The whole scenario could have been an illusion.
Did he hear, see, or smell something wrong,
Or was the snitch guessing all along?
Where statements are made based just on hearsay,
The anonymous tip doesn't pay its way.
Here, the plan for the road trip can't cure this deficiency,
Since the plan was quite vague and lacked specificity.
There's no probable cause for a warrant whenever
Some folks take a trip and then drive home together."[22]

A Chinese Puzzle

Several Chinese males proved to be inscrutable
To some Keystone Cops who were quite unsuitable.
When agents arrested a man named Hom Wei
For possession of smack, he agreed to play
The part of a snitch, once he got arrested,
Though his trustworthiness had yet to be tested.
He told them his smack came from Blackie Toy,
Whose Chinese laundry had a sign reading "Oye."

Then six narcs hid out while a federal Dick
Employed tactics quite underhanded and slick.
He told Blackie Toy that he drove out there
To retrieve his shirts and outerwear.
Toy replied to the Dick, "We're not open till eight."
But the narcs didn't want to gain entry so late.
The Dick then showed his badge. Toy slammed the door,
And fled to his quarters behind the store.
The agents broke in, and chased Blackie down.
They searched his bedroom, but no drugs were found.
Nonetheless, they arrested Blackie Toy,
Slapping on handcuffs in front of his boy.
They told Toy they'd spoken to Hom Wei,
Who said Toy sold him smack the prior day.
Toy insisted, "No, *I* haven't sold any,
But I know who did, and his name is Johnny.
I smoked some smack with him yesterday
At his house, which isn't far away."

They took Toy in tow, and found Johnny's place.
Johnny handed the smack over face-to-face.
He told them he got it from Toy and Wong Sun.
Narcs saw there was more work that had to be done.
Toy showed them the dwelling of Mr. Wong Sun,
Who was sleeping in bed when narcs slapped the cuffs on.
But although they searched for quite awhile,
No drugs were found in Wong's domicile.

Wong and Toy went to court that very same day,
And both bonded out without any delay.
It was not until several days later
That each met with an interrogator.
Despite being warned they did not have to speak,
Each one told his story, somewhat tongue-in-cheek.

Would the Court find the officers' entry unlawful,
And Blackie Toy's bedroom arrest just as awful?
At the heads of the Feds, the Court hurled a torrent
Of critiques for their failure to get any warrant.
The Court added, "They also lacked probable cause
For a warrant, had they thought to follow the laws.
While there is a rule giving grounds for arrest
Based on tips from a snitch who's been put to the test,
That rule did not fit in the present case --
No judge would okay the raid on Toy's place.

"Did narcs screw up the case so dramatically
That we are obliged to set all these men free?
Statements derived from an unlawful entry
Can't be used, since they came from illegality.
This taints all the evidence gained as its fruit,
Like the leads Toy gave narcs during the pursuit.
Therefore, the smack traced to Johnny Yee
Is the fruit of that poisonous tree,
And can't be admitted to convict Mr. Toy
When his bedroom statements were obtained through a ploy.

"As for Mr. Wong Sun, he too was arrested
Without probable cause. That can be attested.
But could his confession and/or denial
Be used as evidence against him at trial?
By the time he confessed, the taint had dissipated.
The connection had grown too attenuated.
We'll allow Wong Sun's statements to come in --
Let the jury decide which side will win.

Plus, the smack seized at the home of Yee
Did not invade Wong Sun's privacy.
Feds may use the smack to corroborate
The facts Wong Sun admitted to the State."[23]

Cost-Benefit Versus the Constitution

When the cops set their sights on Alberto Leon,
They had only an unverified tip to go on.
Their snooping gave them a little more info,
Though it did not suffice for them to go
And seek warrants to grab a long list of stuff
From three homes and four cars. They had not snooped enough.
In fact, the police lacked probable cause
To believe Leon and his friends broke the laws,
Since the activities viewed by the cops built
A case for innocence as much as for guilt.
Did they fudge when they went to a magistrate,
Hoping that trusting jurist would take the bait?
The local judge granted their applications
To search for drugs at all seven locations.

The state's courts held, "The D.A. cannot use
The seized evidence, since when cops abuse
Their position by seeking a warrant that's defective,
It undermines the Fourth Amendment's objective."

The High Court declined to take a look
To see whether the warrant went by the book.
Said the Court, "We have the power to ignore that question
And decide another, at the D.A.'s suggestion.
So instead, we have opted to decide:
Should the Exclusionary Rule be modified?

"When the cops did their searching, it was in reliance
On a court-approved warrant. That showed their compliance.
Why should they be punished if the warrant fell short?
Their good-faith reliance was not a tort.
If we weigh the benefits and the cost
Of suppressing the evidence, too much is lost.
When the courts forbid a D.A. to use

YOUR RIGHTS WHEN STOPPED BY POLICE

Nancy E. Albert

All the evidence, that is not what we choose.
So we hereby revise the Rule of Exclusion.
We've hardly eroded its primary function
By allowing this evidence to come in
Where the cops themselves committed no sin.
After all, the rule was meant to deter
Wayward cops, not courts. That's what we infer.
This way, we've balanced the goals of society
Against a modest reduction in privacy.
So today, we establish a 'Good-Faith Exception,'
And announce the Exclusion Rule's modification."

The dissenters were nothing less than incredulous --
They considered the broad new exception dangerous.
"Must this ill-suited cost-benefit analysis
Infect our thinking to the point of paralysis?
Though it may seem cathartic,
It's much like a narcotic.
It draws us into a curious land
That frankly, we cannot understand,
Where the cost of exclusion rises quite high, and
The benefits vanish with a wave of the hand.
These self-styled mystics
Claim to use statistics
To prove that society
Would be better off if we
Simply forfeit our rights,
And give cops green lights.
This Business School theory creates the illusion
That costs have been measured with great precision.
In fact, the government's own studies show
The costs of exclusion to be quite low.

"Courts and cops are not constitutional strangers --
They work hand-in-hand to confront common dangers.
Courts can't be absolved of responsibility,
Since they are part of the system's machinery.
This was nothing less than a naked invasion
Of defendants' homes without justification.

If we want to remain a just society,
We must not give in to expediency.
The decision announces the strangulation
Of a key protection -- the Rule of Exclusion."[24]

Rights in Remission

Mark Anderson was present at the station
The day Bennie Herring shared his suspicion
With the D.A. that Investigator Anderson
Was involved in the killing of a young person.
Mark urged him to drop the accusation,
But Herring stuck to his allegation.

Because Herring said that he wouldn't budge,
Anderson continued to harbor a grudge.
One afternoon, in two thousand four,
Herring showed up at the station's door.
He'd come to retrieve some belongings
From a truck they'd impounded containing his things.
When Anderson learned that his nemesis
Had arrived in person on the premises,
Anderson did not even hesitate
To devise a way to retaliate.
He asked the Department's warrant clerk,
"Are there warrants outstanding for that jerk?"
When she told him no, he replied, "What the heck,
Call the county next door, and ask them to check."
The clerk she phoned looked at her own CRT,
And reported her finding with certainty:
"There's a warrant outstanding. He failed to appear
On a felony charge, filed early this year."

Anderson and a deputy rushed to the spot
Where Herring remained in the impoundment lot.
Bennie Herring became extremely distressed
When the pair searched him incident to his arrest,
Since they found some meth right on his person,
And by searching his truck, they found a gun.
Minutes later, the cops were quite appalled
When they learned the warrant had been recalled.
The database was five months out of date,
And the clerk discovered the defect too late.

In court, Bennie Herring's legal eagle
Argued that the arrest was illegal,
So the gun, plus the meth found near his chest
Were required by law to be suppressed.
But the trial judge said, with a wave of the hand,
"Based on Leon's case, we must all understand:
Since cops made the arrest in a good-faith belief
That the warrant was good, I can't grant that relief."

Did the negligent act of an employee
Working for cops in a nearby county
Mean the evidence ought to be suppressed
When seized as the fruit of a faulty arrest?
Would the Fourth Amendment Rule of Exclusion
Bring the matter to a swift conclusion?

Justice John Roberts spoke for the Court
In a 5-4 decision, and filed this report:
"When the Court announced the Exclusionary Rule,
We intended that it be used as a tool
To deter police, since we saw a torrent
Of arrests and searches without a warrant.
But we never intended that it should be
A way for offenders to get off scot-free.
It's one thing in cases where cops intended
Some wrongdoing that cannot be defended.
But here, their actions were so innocent --
We must find a way to be munificent.
The screw-up was somewhat *dehors* the loop
That landed this defendant in the soup.
This arrest can be traced to an actor
For whom ill intent was not a factor.
And so, for the case we decide today,
The Rule of Exclusion does not pay its way.
The benefit does not exceed the cost.
Therefore, Bennie Herring's case must be lost."

Some observers found the holding arbitrary --
To them, it sounded like an obituary.

Might the Rule of Exclusion gradually
Shrivel up and become part of history?

Justice Ruth Bader Ginsburg wrote for the four
Dissenters who wanted the Rule to do more:
"The majority fails to comprehend
That without the Rule, there's no way to mend
Abuses endured at the hands of police.
The Rule and Amendment belong in one piece.
Now, innocents will have no insulation
From sloppy records at a police station.
Enforcing the Rule of Exclusion's a must,
Since it's needed to gain the public's trust.
This arrest was due to a cop's motivation
To legitimate his own predisposition.
Judges should not put themselves in the position
Of partnership in a nefarious mission.
The Rule of Exclusion is the only deal
In town that can make Fourth Amendment rights real.
We should not give the police permission
To put our treasured rights into remission."[25]

Pooch on the Porch

The place was deadly quiet. There was no one on the lawn.
No cars were in the driveway, and the blinds were tightly drawn.
But someone left the cops a tip that somewhere on that lot,
Joelis Jardines might be busy growing pot.
When it came to specifics, the tipster gave too few
To justify a sound belief that the tip was true.

Two detectives went investigating with man's best friend.
Ole Franky sniffed and sniffed to sense which way the trail might wend.
The process didn't take long -- just a minute or two.
It just depended on which way the fickle wind blew.
When he jumped up on the porch, Franky's search came to an end.
Once he alerted at the door, his posture did portend
That the drugs good ole Franky was well-trained to detect
Were right inside the house, which cops needed to inspect.

Cops went and got a warrant. Then they found pot plants galore.
Plants on the tables and the chairs and even on the floor.
Jardines was arrested and charged with a major crime.
If convicted, he would have to serve a lot of time.
But at trial Jardines said, "This is a situation
Where police can't use the pot due to their violation.
The dog sniff was a 'search' where cops had no right to be,
Since one's home includes the porch along with the front entry."

The Court acknowledged it had ruled in prior dog sniff cases,
But all of those had taken place in very public places.
So the Jurists chose to analyze Amendment Number Four
To see if the Framers meant to ban a dog sniff near one's door.

The vote came close, with just one Member's vote to spare.
Said five Jurists, "The cops should never have been there
If their visit was for the purpose of snooping,
Let alone with a helper that might be pooping.
You've a right to be free from the Government's gaze
In your home and environs, which we call 'curtilage'.
Thus, when agents closed in with four feet and four paws
They were brazenly breaking no-trespassing laws.

"Your home is where you have a right to be.
There's a transgression here that's plain to see.
One's home is at the rule's very core,
So no spying from porches any more.
The law is clear, and it's really quite easy --
There is a bright line that protects property."[26]

Snooping with Sensors

The challenge resembled a Gordian knot.
Agents placed their bets on a rather long shot
In order to figure out whether or not
Danny Kyllo was using his home to grow pot.

Danny lived in a home on a lovely lane,
Where no telltale signs could be seen from a plane.
So the Feds decided to see what they could see
By employing some modern technology.
They chose a thermal-imaging device
After getting some scientific advice
About measuring heat that emanated,
Which using heat lamps might have generated.
They thought they could manage to garner some proof
If they measured the heat that rose from his roof.

Would thermal emissions
Confirm their suspicions?
Well, much to the Feds' delight and surprise,
The thermograms proved a sight for sore eyes.
They showed that Danny's roof was a lot
Hotter than neighbors' who didn't grow pot.
They rushed their results to a magistrate,
To get a warrant before it was too late.
Then they searched the home, and found what they'd suspected --
A hundred pot plants -- about what they'd projected.

Danny claimed, "They're allowed to use their sight
To view any telltale signs that they might,
But I have a Fourth Amendment guarantee,
That they cannot intrude on my privacy.
The use of that gizmo to measure the heat
Gave the Feds a sneaky, lawless way to cheat."

The Nine would decide, from their exalted perch,
Did using that gizmo constitute a search

For purposes of the Fourth Amendment,
Thus requiring Feds to get a warrant?
"We do not like the use, forsooth,
Of wiretaps on a telephone booth.
We've said it's fine to use a plane
To spot what info cops could gain.[27]
As long as cops just use their eyes,
We're not about to criticize.

"But should we just sit by as technology
Devours the domain of our privacy?
Sense-enhancing gizmos should not be allowed
To peer into places hidden from a crowd.
If the place is not in public use,
For intruding, there is no excuse.
When the Fourth Amendment first got adopted,
Framers couldn't predict what might get co-opted.
The rule we select must accommodate
Technologies even more up-to-date.
Things that see through walls make us wary,
Since they're feasible and awfully scary.
The Fourth Amendment draws a very bright line
At the door of the home, and to us, that's just fine.
So based upon our extensive research,
We find imaging was an unlawful search."[28]

Court to Big Brother: About GPS

Antoine Jones was a businessman. It was his job to run
A trendy little nightclub where politicos went for fun.
His problems all began by a strange fortuity
When his partner Larry drew the gendarmes' scrutiny.
In a traffic stop for speeding, K-9s sniffed drug residue.
Then the cops found wads of Franklins that were hidden out of view.

The car belonged to Jones, so cops pegged him as their dude,
But their plan to pin a crime on him he managed to elude.
They used each tactic that they had in their police toolkit,
But wiretaps and cameras didn't yield a single hit.
A mastermind conspirator was who they thought he was.
He's kingpin of a drug ring, or so believed the fuzz.

"How is it that we know it
But yet can't seem to prove it?"
The cops said that a lot
Until they came up with a plot.
"We'll get a warrant from a judge -- that'll do the trick,
And use GPS to track him. Now wouldn't that be slick?"

But the problem was that by the time they reached his neighborhood,
And stuck the doodad on his car, the warrant was no good.
Well, the GPS worked perfectly; it tracked him day and night.
For four weeks straight, where'er he went, they had him in their sight.
Then the Feds pieced all the data into a large mosaic
Which showed that Jones's lifestyle was not the least prosaic.

Like his visits to a crack house where cops later found a stash,
And confiscated close to a million bucks in cash.

Still, they couldn't prove a link to Jones, and wondered what to do.
So they charged him with a drug crime, and threw in conspiracy, too.
The Feds took Jones to trial for dealing in coke,
And when the trial was over, the jury spoke:
"Not guilty on drug trafficking, and on conspiracy,
We're hung; there's not enough here to convict this detainee."

The Feds had one remaining card they opted to play --
Retrying him for conspiracy another day.
This time the Feds got their way; so after all that strife,
The jury found him guilty, and Jones wound up with life.

But Jones said, "Hold your horses; that evidence is awful,
'Cause all of it was gotten by a method that's unlawful.
The Court must exclude the tracking data that it used against me,
Since the Fourth Amendment bans intrusions on my privacy."

For the nine High Court Justices, the case hit a nerve.
The extent of police intrusion threw them a curve.
Thoughts about their own cars made it personal --
Could the cops track *their* movements *sans* court approval?

To some of the Nine, tracking a short trip was fine,
But four full weeks of tracking simply crossed the line.
"So what should we do?" They debated the question,
"Is warrantless tracking just too much intrusion?
This new means of spying is far too revealing;
All our private data the State could be stealing."

One thing they agreed on: police went too far
By placing or leaving that thing on his car.
"It's either a search or a trespass," they said,
"Whatever the reason, this charge should be dead.
The constables blundered; thus, we agree,
The time has arrived to set this man free."[29]

Privacy in a Digital Age: Cell Phone Searches

What caught the cop's eye was the license plate,
Which appeared to be seriously out-of-date.
Soon after, the driver got apprehended,
As his driving privilege had been suspended.
When the cop searched him incident to the arrest,
Riley, the driver, grew deeply distressed.

The search revealed Riley's gang affiliation,
And that fact was not the sole revelation.
The cop confiscated Dave Riley's smart phone.
Suddenly, the search became truly full-blown.
Detectives found pics linking Dave to a gang crime
That could send him away for a very long time.

Defense counsel cried foul,
And proceeded to growl
That the search of Dave's cell
Did not sit very well --
It did not comply with the Fourth Amendment,
Cuz the fuzz had failed to obtain a warrant.
All that phone info needed to be suppressed
For failing to meet the due process test.

Said the D.A., "The Court in *Robinson*
Carved out this important exception:
Cops may conduct a full search of a person,
Though arrested for a mere traffic transgression."[10]

Would the Court go along, without protest
When cops search cell phones incident-to-arrest?
Lower courts were split over yea or nay,
So this is what the High Court had to say:
"Robinson's license had long been revoked
Before the cops pinched him; then, prodded and poked
Him until, in his coat, they found a cig pack
Full of capsules containing white powder smack.
We decided that searching him was permissible

Because prior cases had found it admissible
When a search is made incident to an arrest --
A principle we did not care to contest.

"Should the *Robinson* rule apply to technology,
And undermine what is left of our privacy?
If Martians were to land on earth,
They might conclude, for what it's worth,
The devices we humans cradle close by,
Are part of our bodies, like an arm or thigh.
We use them so many times each hour
That some folks take them into the shower.

"Is searching a cell phone
Like bugging a pay phone,
Or like searching the wallet
You keep in your pocket?
A rule that applies to a physical object
Loses force when applied to digital content.
A cell phone neither places cops at risk,
Nor destroys evidence gleaned from a frisk.
Unlike wallets, it contains vast quantities
Of data quite valuable to the police.

"Before cell phones, a search was a narrow intrusion.
But now, cops can access a profusion
Of data that invades a person's privacy.
Exempting such searches borders on lunacy.
We think viewing one's browsing history
Resembles perusing one's diary,
Or ransacking a person's whole apartment,
Which is just what the Framers sought to prevent.
Henceforth, cops must get a warrant to meet this Court's test
Before searching a phone seized incident to arrest."
The Nine Justices spoke with a single voice,
Leading civil libertarians to rejoice.[30]

YOUR RIGHTS WHEN STOPPED BY POLICE — Nancy E. Albert

When Is a K-9's Sniff up to Snuff?

He wasn't gunning the engine full blast --
Caballes was driving just six miles too fast.
That made it legit when a highway cop
Pulled him to the curb for a traffic stop.

He forked over the usual documents --
License, registration, proof of insurance.
Then the cop did something that's fairly routine --
He asked the dispatcher, "Is his record clean?"
The cop planned to detain him just long enough
To write up a warning, and not seem too tough.

A nearby trooper hearing the transmission
Rushed to the scene on a fishing expedition.
Despite lack of grounds to think things weren't fine,
The trooper brought his drug-detection canine.
He walked his dog next to the vehicle's trunk,
And the dog alerted like he'd smelled a skunk.
Then the cops searched the trunk without consent.
When they found pot, the officers went
And arrested Caballes for a drug crime.
It all went down in less than ten minutes time.

In court, the man's lawyer moved to suppress
The seized evidence, and to quash his arrest:
"The sniff was a search that was not up to snuff,
Since the troopers lacked grounds to search for the stuff.
A traffic stop can't become a drug investigation
Before there's a basis for reasonable suspicion.
There was no proof that cops smelled a pot smell,
Or had any facts whereby they could tell
That the car that was speeding and got caught
Was likely to be transporting pot."

The trial judge said this of the suspect's detention:
"The stop wasn't prolonged by the cops' intervention,
And the dog sniff provided probable cause

To search the car without breaking the laws."
Then the trial court decided to confine
The man for twelve years, and impose a fine.

The case eventually made its way
To the Top Court, to see what it would say
About whether, in a run-of-the-mill traffic stop,
It's OK, *sans* suspicion, to use a K-9 prop.

The Supreme Court noted that it would be wrong
In a traffic stop to detain one too long,
For detention becomes an unlawful seizure
When it's prolonged beyond a reasonable measure.
The Court ruled, "Where a stop was otherwise lawful,
Adding a canine sniff is not so awful
That it violated the driver's privacy.
Thus, the intrusion was not a travesty."

Two Justices, in dissent, said, "Nope;
The dog search unlawfully broadened the scope,
Since the traffic stop bore no rational connection
To using a dog for drug detection."[31]

A Sniff Too Late

A K-9 cop and his trained dog Floyd
Reacted to the following factoid --
A driver strayed onto the shoulder
For a second or two, which made the cop smolder.
It was midnight, so the cop could not observe
Any object that might make the driver swerve.

The cop made a stop of the Mountaineer,
And asked Dennys Rodriguez, "Why did you veer?"
"Not to worry," said he. "It's under control.
I swerved to avoid a gigantic pothole."
The cop deemed the stop an invitation
To demand his license and registration.
Then the officer ran a records check
To make sure his background was up to spec.
Though he found no grounds to extend the stop,
The officer called for a back-up cop.
The cop started a round of questioning,
Then handed Rodriguez a written warning.
But the cop would not let Rodriguez leave,
Since he still had something else up his sleeve.

"Is it okay to walk my dog around
Your car? He's a harmless, friendly hound."
Rodriguez declined, and shook his head. "No --
It's quite late, and I really have to go."
But the cop ignored his lack of consent.
He let Floyd out, and around the dog went.
It took only eight minutes -- a minor delay.
But in that decision, Rodriguez had no say.
The dog alerted to the presence of meth,
And a search of the car spelled the kiss of death.

Rodriguez got charged with a drug offense,
And moved to suppress the evidence.
Defense counsel said the cop mustn't prolong
The stop without grounds to suspect any wrong.

The lower courts ruled: "We've heard enough about this.
A time lag of eight minutes is *de minimis*."

But the High Court looked at the facts and said,
"What part of *Caballes* have they not read?
This stop was like a *Terry*-type detention.
Such stops must be quite brief, we need to mention.
Once a ticket's given out, the cop's mission is complete.
So the sniff must not be added by the cop on the street.
Amendment Four bans a new investigation
That lengthens the time of the roadside detention."[32]

YOUR RIGHTS WHEN STOPPED BY POLICE — Nancy E. Albert

Consent-Searches

At three in the morning
Without any warning,
Officer Rand, a Sunnyvale cop,
Made a legitimate traffic stop.
"Your light is burned out. Can I see your I.D.?"
Said Rand to the driver, who readily
Admitted that he had no license to show.
Then the guy beside him spoke through the window.

"I've got a license," said the guy named Joe.
He seemed willing to help *ab initio*.
"This car belongs to my family --
It was my brother who lent it to me."
Six Hispanic males were seated inside.
When two backup cop vehicles pulled astride,
The six exited the car, one by one
At Officer Rand's kind invitation.

Then Rand said to Joe,
"Do you mind if I go
"In the car and take a look inside?"
"Sure," said Joe. "I've got nothing to hide."
So cops entered the car and looked around,
And beneath the rear seat they quickly found
And just as quickly confiscated
Some checks that had been liberated.
The blank checks came from a local Speedway
Car Wash office burgled on a prior day.
Bob Bustamonte, who sat in the front seat,
Had been using the checks to steal and to cheat.
Cops searched through his cars, parked away from the scene.
They found more blank checks, plus a check-writing machine.

Bob went to trial on a charge that outlawed
Possession of checks with intent to defraud.

YOUR RIGHTS WHEN STOPPED BY POLICE — Nancy E. Albert

In court, defense counsel moved to exclude
The evidence of his turpitude,
For without the goods, there'd be no case
On which his conviction could be based.
Counsel insisted the search was no good,
Since they never proved that Joe understood
That the law provides each of us with the right
To withhold our consent without causing a fight.

A hearing took place in an effort to query
If Joe's consent to the search was voluntary.
"When I asked the six males to step out of there,"
Said the cop, "It was a congenial atmosphere.
I never threatened the men with arrest,
As the driver of the car will attest."
The driver supported the officer's story
That the cop had done nothing inflammatory.

The trial court agreed, and Bob got convicted,
But state and federal courts were conflicted --
Should consent be considered voluntary
In the face of optics to the contrary?
Did the strobe lights and guns prove the assertion
That cops used a subtle form of coercion?
A federal court dealt the trial court a blow
By ruling the cops should have advised Joe
That he had the right to freely withhold
His consent to a search and turn them down cold.

Could the Fourth Amendment save Joe's friend's skin?
The U.S. Supreme Court commenced to weigh in:
"Now it's always been true that under our laws
A search needs a warrant and probable cause.
But for years we've assumed that there's an exception
Where the subject consents at his own election.
What we need to know is what D.A.s must show
To prove Joe's consent was willing, not *faux*.

"Is a cop's advisement the *sine qua non*,

Or is that something we need not rely on?
Lest skeptics speculate, all atwitter,
Here are some factors we would consider:
The subject's youth, schooling, and I.Q.,
Prolonged questioning, and beatings, too.

"We must treat this case with the most careful scrutiny,
Since brutality defeats a consent's validity,
And we'll note subtly coercive police actions
While observing an impaired subject's reactions.

"But informing a subject of the right to refuse
Would impair the ability of cops to use
Consent-searches as an investigative technique,
And render police powers altogether too weak.
Consent-searches are part of a cop's stock-in-trade --
That's how lots of successful searches are made.

"Each search comes with its own facts and fluidity,
So we must view the facts in their totality.
As long as the suspect is not held in custody,
A consent-search *sans* coercion has validity."

Three dissenters said, "Consent should be a 'knowing choice';
Without knowing his options, the subject lacks a voice.
If he didn't know he could refuse assent,
Joe had no way to knowingly consent.
When our brethren talk about practicality,
What they really mean is the ability
Of cops to do searches while evading
Limits the law says they should be obeying.
Since the Feds advise folks they've a right to refusal,
Why should local cops claim it's too impractical?
This case sanctions a game of blindman's bluff.
It's wrong to say that this is fair enough."[33]

Passengers Park Their Rights at the Curb

One can sum up this case with the following blurb:
Auto passengers park their rights at the curb.
In a home, folks can look to the Fourth Amendment,
But courts have concluded that cars are different.
Compared to vehicles, the fact is, forsooth,
You've more right to privacy in a phone booth.

An armed robbery went down one frigid night.
Two masked robbers lost no time in taking flight.
The cops got a call before they'd gone far,
Describing in broad terms the getaway car.

Cops spotted a car that looked about right,
And stopped the car to impede its flight.
They ordered the riders to step outside,
And searched it to see if they'd something to hide.
One of the riders was a man named Rakas,
And when cops searched the car, he raised a fracas.
What cops uncovered was no small trifle --
A box of bullets and a sawed-off rifle.

In court, defense counsel moved to suppress
The gun and the bullets from evidence.
He argued the search of the car was illegal.
"You've got to exclude it," said the legal eagle --
"There were insufficient grounds for the cop
To make a legitimate traffic stop."

But the trial judge decided not to bend,
Since the car belonged to one suspect's girlfriend,
And mere passengers who get caught in the lurch
Have no standing to complain of the search.
Since the judge held the men had no right to complain,
He had no occasion to try and explain
Whether or not the stop and search complied
With the arguments for the passengers' side.

When they lost their case in the courts below,
The passengers, with their lawyer in tow,
Asked the High Court to broaden the rule,
And give standing to passengers as a tool.
Said the Court, "We'll decide if it's necessary
For passengers to claim a possessory
Interest to urge that the Fourth Amendment
Bans searching the passenger compartment."

Perhaps the fates did not bode in their favor,
As the perps evoked an unsavory flavor.
The Court found a lack of legitimacy
To the perps' claims of a right to privacy
In a car belonging to someone not them.
That proved an insurmountable problem.
The Court declined to exclude the evidence,
Since they had no valid Fourth Amendment defense.
The claim of these passengers had to fail
Without privacy rights in the automobile.

Four dissenters exclaimed, "This invites a cop
To willy-nilly search and stop
Any car with more than one rider inside
Without the Fourth Amendment as a guide.
"We think," they said, "A rule is too feeble
That safeguards property in lieu of people."[34]

Rousting the Riders

In *Mimms*, the Court said without equivocation:
When a car's stopped for a traffic violation,
Cops can tell the driver to stand outside
Because *Terry* said safety concerns trump pride.
So where do passengers fit in this mix?
Should a traffic stop leave them in a fix?
Is rousting passengers merely incremental?
Is the toll on their freedom more fundamental?

Jerry Lee Wilson became an outcast
When his driver got stopped for going too fast.
Fifty-five was the limit, if we're keeping score,
And the driver was doing sixty-four.
The cop noticed Jerry starting to sweat,
And guessed this was someone he needed to vet.
The cop ordered Jerry out of the sedan.
Though he'd done nothing wrong, he obeyed the man.
When Jerry stood up, some drugs fell down,
And the cop's friendly smile became a frown.

He then placed Jerry under arrest.
Jerry moved to have the drugs suppressed.
If the car was stopped for the *driver's* offense,
Did ordering Jerry out make any sense?
If the order breached Jerry's Fourth Amendment right,
The drugs would be suppressed and never come to light.

The nine High Court Justices could not agree
On the right of passengers to liberty,
Absent evidence that passengers pose a threat.
Should a threat be a threshold that needs to be met?
Is it kosher to force them from their comfort zone
To stand out in bad weather, for reasons unknown?

Said the Court, "It's always a balancing test
To decide for the country which course is best
When weighing the rights of an average guy

Versus shielding a cop lest things go awry.
One might not expect a violent reaction
Where the crime involved is a traffic infraction,
But the danger increases when there is more
Than one person the cop needs to watch out for --
The potential for harm
Could be cause for alarm.
So for the first time, we draw this conclusion:
Telling all to get out is not too much intrusion."

Two dissenting Justices used a different scale.
They said, "The passenger's interest should prevail,
Since during a routine traffic stop
There's negligible risk to the traffic cop,
But the burden on thousands of people is obvious --
To them, the government's intrusion is odious.
Standing out in the street is a situation
That causes the innocent humiliation.
Today's decision condones a seizure
Based on no suspicion whatsoever."[35]

An Exit for Passengers

In *Rakas*, cops rushed to the scene of a crime,
And waylaid a car in the nick of time.
When the passengers claimed a right to suppress
What cops found in the car, they had no redress.
The claim of the passengers had to fail
Because they did not own the automobile.[36]

So do passengers lose all their rights
If officers get them in their sights?
Some cops spotted a car they opted to stop,
Though their rationale really didn't hold up.
When they spied Bruce Brendlin sitting inside,
Police knew the guy had something to hide,
Since they knew Bruce as one of two men
That they had seen again and again.
A parole violation put Bruce in jeopardy,
So police officers took him into custody.
They conducted a search incident to the arrest,
And found drug paraphernalia close to his vest.
He didn't complain of cops' search of the car --
It was the search of his person that went too far.
"Cops can't stop a car for no good reason,"
The passenger claimed. "There's no open season
On stopping cars without grounds for suspicion.
These cops ran afoul of the Constitution."

The matter wound up in the nation's High Court,
And the Justices wrote a nine-zero report
On a passenger's right to challenge a stop
When it's made without grounds by a traffic cop.
They said, "A traffic stop is a 'seizure,'
Since none are free to leave at their leisure,
And the Fourth Amendment forbids the detention
Of driver and guest without justification.
Since the evidence stemmed from a stop based on a whim,
Brendlin had a right to challenge its use against him.

We won't okay a stop based on *Terry*
Where police behavior is arbitrary."[37]

Passenger Pat-Downs

Do the cops in a traffic stop go too far
When they tell a passenger, "get out of the car,"
And then proceed to frisk the man?
Does that transgress a Fourth Amendment ban?
We saw what happened to Jerry Lee -- [38]
This case further erodes one's security.

A traffic stop is often very
Like the stop-and-frisk in *Terry* --
It's rather brief and temporary
And for the cops it can be scary.
Terry said a stop-and-frisk has two requirements,
And can't pass muster without both elements:
For the stop -- grounds to believe a crime's taking place,
For the frisk -- signs the person has a gun someplace.

But how can cops tell if a person is dangerous
And more apt to be armed than most of the rest of us?
Should the cops be granted additional leniency
To stop-and-frisk when inside of gang territory?

Three gang task force officers were on patrol
In a Crips-infested hood they had chosen to troll.
They spotted a car in the dark of the night,
But could not see inside due to lack of light.
They saw no signs of criminal activity,
But due to the hood, they presumed a proclivity.
Sparks started to fly with the cops' abrupt action
In stopping the car for a civil infraction --
A plate check revealed the insurance had ended,
And the car's registration had been suspended.

During the stop, a cop named Maria
Peered into the car and got an idea.
The back-seat passenger wore a blue bandana,
And in his pocket she saw a scanner.
These facts and Lemon's overall manner

Led her to believe he might be a gang member.
"Get out of the car," she shouted to Lemon,
Then patted him down to check for a weapon.
It felt like a gun somewhere near his waist,
And she slapped on the cuffs with all due haste.

Lemon complained that the search was the fruit
Of a groundless detention, and to boot,
The Fourth Amendment's restriction precludes
A pat-down when a cop wrongly intrudes.

But the High Court decided, nine to none
That in this case, the cops had won.
"Provided it doesn't extend the duration
Of the traffic stop, we find no violation.
So long as it's a lawful traffic stop,
We'll allow passenger pat-downs by a cop.
If she thinks the guy's armed, the pat-down's permitted
Without her belief that a crime was committed.
Never mind an innocent passenger's sensitivity.
It's the cop's fear of danger that rules our activity."[39]

Searches Limited by Time and Space

This story began in a dark basement lair
With a snitch who saw a chrome handgun down there.
He told the police when he started to chat
He'd bought drugs there from Polo, a black dude who was fat.
Police sought a warrant to search for the rod
In that tiny apartment low-slung near the sod.

When they got the warrant, it was well nigh nine at night,
And cops wished to start searching as soon as they might.
In an unmarked car, two detectives sat in wait
For the search team to show up and enter the gate.
They watched two men exit upstairs, unaware
Of the search warrant or the detectives' snare.

The two men drove off, neither giving a hoot
That police were following in hot pursuit.
Detectives tailed them, and at their leisure,
Forced them out of the car, and that was a seizure.
The cops seized the pair for no violation --
The stop was based purely on their speculation
That the men, who fit the snitch's rough description
Might split ere they could manage the situation.

Cops cuffed them, but said they weren't under arrest --
Just detained till the proceeds became manifest.
In the meantime, the search team, armed with the warrant
Found drugs and the gun in the basement apartment.
But nothing was found in the search of the men,
Save a key linking Bailey to the basement den.
Then the Feds threw the book at "Polo" Bailey,
Based on the drugs, gun, and the basement door key.

In court, Bailey saw himself as a victim,

Since cops lacked the right to stop or detain him.
"The evidence came from an illegal stop --
That's abuse of power by a misguided cop,"
He argued. But the judge said the stop wasn't abhorrent
Since his seizure was incident to a lawful warrant.
A jury found him guilty. He got thirty years in jail,
But the Supreme Court took the case, and Bailey asked for bail.

Then the Supremes, by a vote of six to three
Reversed the conviction of Polo Bailey.
Said the Court, "You can hold folks standing next to the place
Being searched. Years ago, we decided that case.
But here, they'd traveled a mile from the site
Before cops swooped down to prevent their flight.
The search of the basement had not even started
Before these two men had long since departed.

"If we let cops grab those outside the vicinity,
Could they stop folks all the way up to infinity?
That would give officers too much discretion.
We find this to be an unlawful intrusion.
It's important for cops to gain comprehension
That every search has a spatial dimension."[40]

It Takes Two to Tango

Things had gone so awry between Janet and Scott,
They seemed to regret ever tying the knot.
Janet took their son home to her Mom and Dad,
But then brought him back, though she still felt quite mad.
Scott hid the kid to keep her from removing
Him from the U.S., since Scott was disapproving.
That prompted Janet to call the police.
She told them Scott's antics needed to cease,
Since her husband had been abusing cocaine,
And he had returned to the habit again.
When Scott told the cops, "It's really not me --
She's the addict," she replied, "Come and see.
There's evidence of his use inside.
Come right in; I've got nothing to hide."
But Scott immediately interjected,
"You can't come in. My rights must be respected."

After making sure the boy had been found,
Cops entered the home, and then looked around.
When the cops saw Scott's room, it became plain
That Scott had been actively using cocaine.
But when Scott got indicted and went to court,
He objected, "That evidence comes up short,
Since she lacked the authority to consent
To the search at a time when I was present.
So the proceeds cops took before my arrest
Should not be admitted; they must be suppressed."

If two people reside in a home that is shared,
Can a non-consenting person be spared
From intrusions caused by a warrantless search
Over his objection, and be left in the lurch?
Does a spouse or co-tenant possess the power
To veto the search when their bond has gone sour?

Said the High Court, "What is the Fourth Amendment for
If a guy can't decline when he comes to his door?
There's a widely shared social expectation
That police may not enter over the objection
Of a roommate who, when asked for consent, says no
To a search where the cops have no warrant to show.
If one's roommate objects, there's really no doubt
That the cops can't come in; they have to stay out.
But those who are sleeping or watching TV
Lose their chance to object, and the cops are home-free."[41]

Risky Roommates

This case is imbued with all the drama
Of a stage play full of tears and trauma.
Act One: Lopez cashes a check at a bank.
He has only his lucky stars to thank,
Since he barely escapes with his own precious life
When the bald guy, Fernandez, stabs him with a knife,
Saying, "In case you ain't able to guess,
This hood is ruled by the gang D.F.S."
As Lopez flees, he contacts 911,
But Fernandez's cohorts come on the run.
They knock him down. Then they kick and they bash
Him all over, and grab his cell phone and cash.

Act Two: Cops enter, saying they have no doubt --
This alley is where the gang members hang out.
They spot a scared guy in the alley who said,
"He's in the building you can see straight ahead."
After making sure their backups have arrived,
Cops knock on a door. They hear screaming inside.
The woman who opens the door is Roxanne.
She's crying and bleeding from blows by a man.
She looks like she's feeling a great deal of fear
When a man out of nowhere seems to appear.
It's Fernandez himself who quickly draws near,
And says to the cops, "You can't just barge in here.
I know my rights. You can't have a look-see."
But the cops take him into custody.
Lopez tells the cops, "He's the one who knifed me!"
Then cops cart Fernandez off to the pokey.

Act Three: Cops return one hour after the arrest.
Roxanne comes to the door with a babe on her chest.
"He's in jail now, so we would like your consent,"
The cops say, "to search this entire apartment."
Roxanne gives them leave to search the whole place.
They find a shotgun and the knife in that space.
So Fernandez is charged with robbery

And infliction of domestic injury.

The final act shows a big courtroom scene.
Defense counsel states that the go-between,
Roxanne, lacked the authority to consent
To the officers' search of the apartment.
He articulates the defense position
That the search ran afoul of the Constitution --
Access was denied by Roxanne's cotenant,
So the cops should have gone to get a warrant.
But the judge rules: "The knife and gun can come in,"
And the jury finds Fernandez guilty as sin.

The High Court considered that four-act play,
And the Justices had the final say.
They debated the issues with equanimity,
But never managed to achieve unanimity.
In a prior case the Court had decided,
In a ruling where Jurists were divided,
That consent by one resident simply won't do.
If they're both at the scene, consent must come from two.[41]

In this case, Fernandez had told the cops, "No,"
Before they, for Roxanne's sake, took him in tow.
So was the warrantless search impermissible,
And the fruits of that search therefore inadmissible?
Six Justices ruled, "That last case won't apply,
Since Fernandez was no longer standing by
When Roxanne freely gave her consent
To the cops' search of the apartment.
Since his absence was due to a lawful detention,
The lack of his presence is not worth our attention."
So they let that gang member's conviction ride
By weighing in on the D.A.'s side.

But three other Justices said, "Really?
Remember our old friend, Mister McNeely?
We said warrants are needed to curtail the proclivity

Of police to engage in unchecked activity.
We explained that today's technology
Should rid us of the mythology
That warrants take so long the case gets stale.
They're fast when a cop uses phones or email.
Protecting Roxanne provides no excuse,
Since Roxanne would suffer no further abuse
Once Fernandez was handcuffed and taken away.
This case leaves the Fourth Amendment in disarray.
A cotenant's consent was never meant
To trump the requirement. We hereby dissent."[42]

Home Safety Inspections

Camara owned no real property --
He got by, living as a lessee.
But he held onto his dignity,
And wouldn't kowtow to authority.

One day, he heard a knock on the door
Of his residence, on the ground floor.
An inspector said, "I must see your abode,
Since it might not comply with the Housing Code,
Which forbids residing on the ground floor.
So inspection is what I've come here for."

But Camara found the intrusion abhorrent,
And demanded that the man produce a warrant.
Two days later, the inspector came back,
And Camara said, "You're on the wrong track.
Without a warrant, I won't let you in,
So please do not come back here again."

Did he have to comply
When some unknown guy
Showed up out of the blue,
Or could he say, "Skiddoo"?
May one lodge an objection
To a home safety inspection?

Soon, a citation arrived in the mail.
It looked like the Government would prevail.
It ordered Camara to appear
At the D.A.'s office. That was clear.

When he failed to appear, two inspectors rode
To his home and displayed the Housing Code,
Which provided that a city employee
Had the right to come in to perform his duty.

Camara once again refused,

So a charge was filed that accused
Him of declining to have his home tested.
Then, the city had Camara arrested.

Camara went and filed a petition
Seeking a writ of prohibition,
Saying, "The Housing Code is contrary
To the Fourth Amendment, and quite scary,
Since it violates one's security
By invading one's right to privacy."

The controversy landed in the lap
Of the High Court, which then resolved the flap.
The Nine noted, "There was no emergency
Requiring inspection with such urgency.
A warrant could've been obtained by the city
That would have enabled Camara to see
The need for and limits of the search,
So that he wouldn't feel left in the lurch.
We hold he had a constitutional right
To insist on a warrant to search his site."[43]

Chapter III. Turning the Tables

Fourth Amendment: The right of the people to be secure in their persons, houses, papers, and effects, against unreasonable searches and seizures, shall not be violated, and no Warrants shall issue, but upon probable cause, supported by Oath or affirmation, and particularly describing the place to be searched, and the persons or things to be seized.

Federal Civil Rights Act, Section 1983: Every person who, under color of any statute, ordinance, regulation, custom or usage, of any State or Territory or the District of Columbia, subjects or causes to be subjected, any citizen of the United States or other person within the jurisdiction thereof to the deprivation of any rights, privileges, or immunities secured by the Constitution and laws, shall be liable to the party injured in an action at law, suit in equity, or other proper proceeding for redress ....

Can You Sue a Cop?

In sixty-five, six narcs descended
On Bivens' home, where they upended
Its contents, and threatened to arrest
His whole family. They were quite distressed!
Then in front of his wife and kids, they threw
The cuffs on Bivens. What a huge snafu!
They hauled him away, then booked and interrogated
Him. Due to a strip-search, he felt humiliated.

Narcs had no warrants underpinning their action --
No wonder it provoked an angry reaction.
Once Bivens got the Feds' complaint dismissed,
He felt quite embarrassed and highly dissed.
So he filed a lawsuit in federal court
(Not a state court damages suit, like a tort),
Claiming the raid on his apartment
Ran afoul of the Fourth Amendment,
And that gave him the right to sue
Each of the narcs. It raised a to-do,
Since no one had ever done that before.
The lower courts quickly showed him the door.

If cops who, while showing a lack of concern,
Search your home, *sans* a warrant, from stem to stern,
Or arrest you, while using excessive force --
Could you sue them for damages? Yes, of course!

The High Court said, "There's a remedy
To protect people and property.
The essence of civil liberty
Is protecting folks against injury.
We hold they're entitled to just compensation
If there was a Fourth Amendment violation."[1]

A Modality for Suing a Locality

After America's Civil War ended,
Many problems still cried out to be mended.
Some states tried passing laws to restrict the rights
Of newly freed slaves. Congress had them in their sights.
Those law-makers came up with a splendid solution --
The Fourteenth Amendment to the Constitution.
It restricted the power of any state
To use its law-making to discriminate.

While all that sounded fine and great,
The President lacked a mandate
To deal with groups like the K.K.K.,
Who wanted to still have things their way
By suppressing the rights of those newly freed
Citizens whose rights had to be guaranteed.

So Congress came up with some legislation
That helped the Chief to unify the nation.
The 1871 Civil Rights Act
Gave the President the powers he lacked
To provide citizens with equal protection
And thwart efforts to practice discrimination.
It also gave those whose rights were violated
A way to get financially compensated
In a federal court at a time when a state
Court might be unwilling to cooperate.

But it took until 1978
For the U. S. courts to appreciate
That the average citizen had a way
To make state and local governments pay
When their agents violate the Constitution.
The High Court finally drew that conclusion
When it construed the words "every person"
To include a municipal corporation.[2]

Immunity and Impunity

A Rhode Island state cop was listening in
When somebody mentioned that he had been
At a party where folks were smoking pot.
He asked his superior whether or not
The phone call was adequate proof to support
A warrant to nab them and take them to court.
He went to a judge and presented the case
That the party was held at the Briggs's place.
The judge agreed that, based on what the cop attested,
Briggs and all the partygoers could be arrested.
Those prominent members of the community
Got arrested at the first opportunity.

But the grand jury refused to indict,
And then Mr. Briggs decided to fight.
He sued, claiming his Fourth Amendment right
Was breached, since the evidence was so slight.

Did Ed Malley, the Rhode Island cop, break the laws
By requesting a warrant *sans* probable cause?
And if so, should Malley be held to account
By having to pay a substantial amount?
Or when cops break the law with impunity,
Might they hide behind immunity
That shields them from liability --
Does that void accountability?

The Nine agreed to consider this question:
Assuming a cop in Malley's position
Should have known that he was breaking the laws
Because the warrant lacked probable cause,
Is he entitled to immunity
From suits seeking a money remedy?

"It is not enough," said the Court, "to fudge
By saying, 'I took the facts to a judge.'
A cop must rely on his own judgment

When seeking to obtain a warrant.
We can only apply this objective test --
A 'reasonable cop' would know what is best.

"We won't grant 'absolute immunity'
For cops who think they're doing their duty.
But a 'qualified immunity' defense
Will protect cops who show basic competence.
A cop won't be immune if, objectively,
In a suit under Section 1983,
No reasonably competent officer would
Have believed the grounds for the warrant were good.
But if reasonable cops could disagree,
Then he should be given immunity."[3]

Clearly Established Law

Take the case of one Afton Callahan.
He seemed like a very simple man.
He lived in a trailer kept nice and clean,
Which he used to sell methamphetamine.
The cops hired a snitch to make a drug buy,
And gave him a transmitter on the sly,
As well as some marked money to use
For buying the meth as part of a ruse.
The cops waited and proceeded to hide,
While Callahan's daughter let him inside.
Callahan took a big bag from his freezer,
And sold him a one-gram bag as a teaser.
When the snitch signaled the deal was done,
The cops rushed in, and their search had begun.
They went through the place for evidence
That clearly proved the drug dealer's offense.

Callahan quite quickly copped a plea,
But he did it conditionally,
Pending appeal of his quest to suppress
The fruits of the search while he prayed for success.

The appeals court found the goods were the fruit
Of an unlawful search, and then, to boot,
Callahan filed a civil rights suit,
Seeking to gain some additional loot.
He said cops ran afoul of the Fourth Amendment
When they entered his home without a warrant.
He argued that he had a right to be free
From intrusions like their warrantless entry.

Years later, the Top Court undertook to see
If those cops had qualified immunity,
Shielding them from liability
If they had behaved responsibly.
"There's a couple of things we need to decide,"
Said the Court, "Before the end of this ride --

Did the cops offend a constitutional right?
Had the right been established before that night?
If the answer is no to the second question,
Callahan will not have a leg to stand on.

"This is a case where well-meaning cops went
Indoors based on the homeowner's consent
For the snitch to enter. The cops could have believed
It extended to them. They would not have conceived
That several years following this event,
We would hold that one cannot transfer consent.
But the cops in this case can have no liability;
They're entitled to claim qualified immunity,
Since when they went inside, it remained good law,
And a valid conclusion for them to draw.
If the rule he offends is not 'clearly established,'
A cop's bank account cannot be diminished."[4]

Deadly Force

One fall night, after dark, in Tennessee,
The scene became ripe for a tragedy.
Young Edward Garner was only fifteen
When he smashed a home's window while hiding unseen.
He broke into a house that was not his own.
He had no accomplice, but acted alone.
The break-in did not net him a lot --
About ten bucks worth was all he got.

Someone called the cops, who arrived at the scene.
They spotted the lad; the youth looked short and lean.
He began to flee, though cops told him to halt.
He came to a fence, which he started to vault.

Although the lead cop saw no sign of a weapon,
That cop did something that could not be undone.
He aimed his gun straight at Edward's head,
And in less than an hour, the lad lay dead.

Edward's Dad, of course, felt devastated.
In federal court, he initiated
A civil rights suit, thereby launching a fight
Claiming violation of his son's rights.

The cops and the city said the suit was no good,
Since the state had a law providing cops could,
After warning a suspect not to flee,
Use deadly force to achieve custody.
Thus, the cop possessed legal authority,
And had followed his Department's policy.

Could the officer's good-faith reliance
On the law be sufficient compliance,
Granting qualified immunity
To act with unfettered impunity?

The High Court said, "Such a policy,
For Americans, would be heresy.
A statute according powers so broad
Is, under the Fourth Amendment, flawed
If it gives cops the right to use deadly force
Against fleeing suspects unless, of course,
The policeman has probable cause to believe
That they pose grave danger if allowed to leave.
It is not better that they all die
Than that they escape while on the fly.
To hold otherwise would be a denial
Of the right to a jury and a trial."[5]

Excessive Force

How can we tell when cops act so aggressive
That their use of force should be deemed excessive?
Should we go with what a cop's gut says is best,
Or should we apply a more objective test?

When Graham felt the onset of a sugar reaction,
He knew he risked running out of time to take action.
He asked Bill Berry to drive him to the store
For some O.J. so he could consume it before
His illness caused him to become comatose --
He needed to offset an insulin dose.

At the store, the waiting line looked far too long.
Graham put back the O.J. and just moved along.
He dashed out of the store, and then he said,
"Please drive me to my buddy's house instead."

When a cop drove up and saw Graham scurry,
He wondered why Graham was in such a hurry.
Without checking the store, the aggressive cop
Executed an investigative stop.
Then he radioed to ask for more
Cops to come while he checked out the store.
Soon, a large group of cops descended --
Their entourage was well-defended.

The back-up cops reacted with indignation
When Bill tried to explain the situation.
"Could you help my sick friend?" Bill Berry said.
But cops opted to brutalize Graham instead.
When he briefly passed out, with a kerplunk,
One cop cursed, "This M.F. is just plain drunk!"
When a friend brought some O.J. to the scene,
Cops kept it from Graham -- they were downright mean.
Then cops checked out the store for the first time,
And learned there never had been any crime.
By the time the ordeal finally came to an end,

Graham had sustained injuries that would not mend.

In court, Graham said cops had used too much force.
They replied, "We're allowed to use force in the course
Of a stop with the goal of investigation
In an evolving, explosive situation,
Unless, when hurting Graham's head, foot and arm,
We acted maliciously to cause him harm."

The High Court said, "No; that is not the rule.
The Fourth's Amendment's our primary tool.
We don't take account of a cop's motivation;
An excessive force case is an objective one --
Were the cops' actions reasonable in the light
Of *all* of the events that took place that night?
The cops must adhere to a three-part guide
When deciding what force may be applied:
How severe was the crime
Suspected at that time?
Did the guy pose a threat
That had to be met?
Did he put up a fight
Or try to take flight
So that cops were not free
To impose custody?
The jury will have to weigh these factors
When sifting through the deeds of the actors."[6]

Driving While Black

Computers should make things better and fairer,
But fail when confounded by human error.
What happened one night in a quaint Texas town
Was something that no one could guess would go down.
The scene that took place there on New Year's Eve
Was so bizarre, it is hard to believe.
A Bellaire cop watching an avenue
Saw a black SUV pull into view.
He entered its license on his keyboard in haste,
Further proving that old adage, "Haste maketh waste."
The plate number matched a stolen SUV,
But it was because he had tapped the wrong key,
And adding to everyone's misery,
That car's profile matched the one he could see.

It pulled into a driveway, and two men got out.
Then the cop grabbed his gun, and started to shout,
"Get down on the ground. I know you're a thief!"
Young Robbie replied, "This is beyond belief.
This is my car, and I live right here."
That young man sounded quite sincere.
The cop seemed to be totally unaware,
The home belonged to a big league ball player.
Robbie's folks emerged when they heard the commotion,
So filled with confusion and emotion.
You could tell they hadn't planned it that way,
Since each parent came out dressed in a p.j.
The cop called for back-up to join him there.
Sergeant Cotton appeared, as if out of thin air.
The Dad told the boys they should obey
The cops and do whatever they say.
Robbie and his cousin lay down on the ground,
And neither of them even uttered a sound.

Robbie's Dad exclaimed, with a sense of pride,
"This is our house; this is where we reside,"
And his Mom offered, "This is a big mistake.

That's our car we allowed our son Robbie to take."
Both sides were feeling exasperated,
And tensions quickly escalated.
Robbie's Mom tried her best to save the day,
But cops felt she was getting in their way.

Then Sergeant Jeffrey Wayne Cotton
Did something extremely rotten.
He shoved her to the garage with such a whack,
She fell to the ground, bruising her arms and back.
Robbie rose to his knees, and with nary a qualm,
Shouted, "Get your fucking hands off my Mom!"
Though the unarmed Robbie sat twenty feet from him,
Cotton shot him through the chest. The prognosis looked grim.
Robbie's dreams for a baseball career were ended,
Since his disabilities could not be mended.

Victims sued the cops, claiming the savage attack
Was all because Robbie was driving while black.
In the lower courts, their case got dismissed.
The courts said the law wasn't well-established.
They ruled that the cops had immunity,
And the right to shoot with impunity,
Since Robbie wore a hoodie that might have concealed
A weapon he might have been likely to wield,
And the cops had grounds to suspect foul play --
Car break-ins had happened the prior day.

The Supreme Court interceded,
Since some cooler heads were needed.
"This case has created so much sound and fury,
The facts need to be sorted out by a jury.
When the facts could favor either side,
We've got to let a jury decide.
So this family's lawsuit is reinstated,
And will have to be fully litigated."[7]

A High-Speed Chase

Don Rickard and Kelly Allen
Had a secret they weren't tellin'.
Whatever that dark secret was,
They wanted to avoid the fuzz.

And yet, at midnight,
With just one headlight,
They drove within sight
Of some cop's strobe light.
So at the corner,
He pulled them over.
He didn't want much --
A license and such.
But Don seemed to freeze
And feel ill at ease.

When he told Don, "Get out,"
Don really freaked out.
Don simply sat tight,
Then quickly took flight.

The cop flipped on the sirens and off he sped,
After the car that was speeding ahead.
Five more cop cruisers joined the chase.
They were roaring at a heady pace.
The gendarmes' hearts were thumping;
Their adrenaline was pumping.
On the I-40 Interstate,
The pursuit began to escalate
As they ramped up the power
To a hundred miles an hour.

In Memphis, Don suddenly veered his car
Onto an exit. He hadn't gone far
When he clipped a cruiser and spun out
A few blocks from the I-40 route.
Then all the cruisers converged.

YOUR RIGHTS WHEN STOPPED BY POLICE
Nancy E. Albert

Surrounding Don's car, they merged.

Guns blazing, several cops drew near.
Don and Kelly, cornered, quaked in fear.
Cops pounded on the window glass,
But Don still tried to take a pass --
He began to back his car away
As a hail of bullets commenced to spray.
Three bullets flew at point-blank range;
Then a dozen more, with no exchange.
The couple seemed to be unarmed.
No way could they escape unharmed.
Cops pummeled Rickard's car with lead.
They got Don and Kelly in the head.
Cops caught it all on video --
It was quite a dramatic rodeo.

When she heard the news, Don's daughter was
dumbfounded.
She thought the use of deadly force was unfounded.
Through her Mom, she said,
"My Father is dead."
She went on to exhort
The federal court:
"If they wanted to detain my pop,
There were less lethal ways to make him stop.
Cops violated Amendment Four
When they fired through the window and the door."

In the case of a minor auto infraction,
Is a high-speed pursuit an over-reaction?
Might the cops simply arrest him later,
After obtaining his license number?
And if cops undertake a hot pursuit,
When is it legit for them to shoot?
If the cops had abstained from pursuing a chase,
Might the risk to the public have been less?

Some courts have found the law to be hazy

On whether it's reasonable or crazy
To use lethal force to keep flight-risks in place
Instead of abandoning the chase.
Should it matter if the original crime
Was small potatoes or something big-time?

While some cities have banned the high-speed chase,
Police practices vary from place to place.
The High Court searched in vain
For cases that made plain
When cops are allowed to commence a pursuit,
And what has to happen before they may shoot.

Justice Alito wrote for the Court
This somewhat brief and halting report:
"The driver acted irresponsibly,
By putting the public in jeopardy.
The officers acted reasonably
In stopping a threat to public safety.
Without countervailing authority,
We must grant the police immunity."

So is this decision a license to kill,
Allowing police to fire at will
On an unarmed suspect who fears the police?
Will it lead to more conflict, or help keep the peace?[8]

Imminent Danger

The high school principal kept her cool
While summoning cops to rush to the school.
The Huff kid had threatened to bring a gun
And use it to shoot up everyone.
"He's been bullied a lot," his classmates said,
"And we really don't want to wind up dead.
We worry more because he's not here;
Is he up to something we should fear?"

The officers shared the high school's worry,
And dispatched to the Huff house in a hurry,
Lest something should happen that all would regret
And folks in the city would never forget.
They knocked on the door and when nobody came,
They announced who they were and one cop said his name.
But no one showed up and no one replied,
So the cops simply stood there, mystified.

Then the Sergeant dialed the Huffs' home phone
To see if the kid might be home alone.
They could hear the phone ring as they waited and all,
But nobody bothered to answer their call.
So rather than waiting or trying to yell,
One cop dialed the number of Mrs. Huff's cell.
Then, lo and behold, he heard Mrs. Huff talk,
And told her, "We're standing out here on your walk."
He wondered if she might be on vacation,
So he asked, "By the way, what is your location?"
She said "I'm inside," sounding rather perturbed.
Then he urged, "Would you speak with us out at the curb?"

She hung up abruptly, but gave no answer.
They stood there wondering, might they be in danger?
Soon she emerged with her young son in tow,
But she never asked, "What do you want to know?"

They told the boy they were there investigating
Some threats at school that had been circulating.
He did not look surprised, nor did he care to chat.
He blurted out, "Did you come here just for that?"

The Sergeant inquired, "Could we talk inside?"
But Mrs. Huff brushed the question aside.
And when he asked, "Are there guns in the house?"
She scampered indoors like a frightened mouse.
The officers did not hesitate --
They followed her in, lest it be too late.
They sensed that this family might be ill-willed,
And they'd seen far too many officers killed.
Then in a flash, Mr. Huff appeared.
"You have to go; you cannot stay here,"
He said, while pointing to the door.
"You can't remain here anymore."

The officers chose a narrow path,
Lest they incur the parents' wrath.
Once the Huffs convinced them the rumors weren't true,
There was a quick exit by the men in blue.
But when the cops left, the Huffs became huffier.
They felt they'd been wronged, and grew even gruffier.
"Our home is our castle, and cops have no right
To barge into our house without an invite.
The Fourth Amendment will serve as our shield
Against entry by cops who will not yield."
So in federal court they chose to fight
The violation of their civil right.

Well, the High Court debated the argument
That cops had to keep out without a warrant.
They pondered the path that the cops had trod,
Noting, "Mrs. Huff's acts were certainly odd.
When the topic of guns joined the conversation,
She fled into the house with no explanation,
And her sudden hang-up -- did she think it a lark,
Or was something rotten in the State of Denmark?

"We can't rely on hindsight and speculate
On the cops' likely jeopardy at the gate.
If they reasonably fear they're in imminent danger
At the hands of some irascible stranger,
The Fourth Amendment will allow a brief entry
In the face of a fast-moving exigency."
The Nine all agreed that the Huffs stood no chance
Of reaping a windfall at the city's expense.[9]

Busted over Seatbelts

Just an ordinary Mom,
Driving along,
Doing no wrong,
Never once guessing that she could possibly
Be treated like someone committing a felony.
Just an ordinary Mom.

But she ran plumb out of luck
As she drove her pick-up truck
With her little girl and boy,
Searching for the girl's lost toy,
When a gung ho Texas cop
Brought her pick-up to a stop.

He appeared to be seething
Because at their last meeting
There was no seatbelt ticket,
Since her group had all clicked it.
He yelled, "We have met before,"
And rushed headlong toward her door,
As he screamed to beat the band,
More than anyone could stand.

She begged, "Please tone it down a decibel --
The kids are frightened and hysterical."
Instead, the officer picked up the pace,
Pointing his finger right in her face.
Then he shouted, "You are going to jail."
At that thought, she turned decidedly pale.

The Mom's major sin --
They weren't belted in.
She'd unbuckled the two
To improve their street view --
A lowly petty crime
That entailed no jail time.

YOUR RIGHTS WHEN STOPPED BY POLICE
Nancy E. Albert

State law gave cops the power to arrest
An offender at a cop's behest,
But it also offered cops the option
In lieu of arrest, to give a citation,
The usual accommodation
For drivers all across the nation.
She appealed to his empathy with the entreat,
"Could I drop off my kids at my friend's down the street?"
"No," he growled, "The kids can go to jail, too."
But her friend showed up for a timely rescue.

The cop handcuffed the Mom, hands behind her back,
And ordered her not to give him any flak.
He forced the kids' Mom into his squad car,
And, ironically, left her seat belt ajar.
At the station, she was searched and booked.
They took her shoes, and officials looked
Through all her belongings, and put her in a cell.
She thought, "How did I get into this kind of hell?"

She pled guilty as charged, and paid her fine,
But was not about to lean back and recline.
She and her spouse went to court and sued
The city and that overreaching dude
Who violated her privacy
By taking her into custody.
Does it make common sense,
Where there's no violence,
To effect an arrest?
They put that to the test.
When the lower courts held their claim fell short,
They took their claim up to the highest court.

Does the Fourth Amendment's guarantee
Protect one from pointless indignity?
The Framers protected the right to be free
Without offering much specificity.
The Jurists looked back in history,

But failed to find unanimity.
All they unearthed was a profusion
Of writings, with no clear conclusion.
So five Members of the High Court's nine
Dodged the question by choosing to decline
To issue a holding that would be conclusive
About whether the arrest was too intrusive.

They agreed that, "On this inauspicious occasion,
The cop imposed gratuitous humiliation.
There was no rationale, like crime prevention,
Nor a compelling need to rush detention.
This couple is asking that we draw the line
Between jailable crimes and those with a fine.
But cops in the field do not have the time
To weigh the severity of each crime.
Although we concede this cop's judgment was poor,
For the moment, we won't impose any cure.
The costs to society could outweigh
The costs to suspects at the end of the day.
Unless there's a rash of pointless arrests,
We believe doing nothing is what seems best."

Justice O'Connor wrote for the four
Jurists who wanted the Court to do more.
She said, "There's already an express guarantee
Against seizures that inflict pointless indignity.
If you look at the words in the Fourth Amendment,
There's no way to come to a contrary judgment.
Five Members today mint a new rule
That we believe is heartless and cruel.
This new rule runs totally contrary
To the core of Due Process history.
It confounds all rationality
To choose clarity above privacy.
The toll on a person's liberty
Is huge when placed into custody.
Where a state says that fines are the punishment,
We should not let cops mete out imprisonment."[10]

Till Sext Do We Part

Jeff Quon, a SWAT team Sergeant, had a rather raunchy quirk
Which first became apparent when he got a fancy perk.
Lieutenant Duke issued Quon a brand new high-tech pager
In hopes that he would use it to make their city safer.
To brief the cops, Lieutenant Duke convened a special meeting
Where he gave the SWAT team members a plain and simple warning:

"Now listen up you guys so you'll be educated:
Foul language on these pagers will not be tolerated.
Know this -- They fall within the city's email policy --
That form you signed says users have no right to privacy.
The city has the right to log and audit your activity,
Since all the info they contain is viewed as city property.
Not only that, you're gonna have to pay a special fee
Any time you overrun the units that are free,
Since it costs the city extra if you exceed the limit,
So please make sure that you will never overuse this gadget.
And one more thing I'll say to you: you'd better pay attention --
It's a thing that I never should even have to mention.
These pagers are for SWAT team work, and that is the extent of it.
You'd better not be texting for your own selfish benefit."

But Quon could not refrain because whenever he felt randy,
He was like a kid let loose in a store full of candy.
He'd text his mistress or his wife so much it was outrageous,
And once Duke saw the bills he thought of docking Jeff Quon's wages.

Duke's ire died down when Quon agreed to pony up the money,
But Quon kept up a deluge of sexting to his honey.

Time after time, Quon failed to heed
The warnings that were stern indeed,
Till Duke's irritation reached such a dimension
That he brought the matter to the Chief's attention.

The Chief said, "Well, we'll just have to see
Why there's so many texts that aren't free.
Did we set the limit way too low,
Or are these cops not tellin' what they know?
An audit is what we will have to do
To see if our allotments are too few.
So we'll ask our carrier for a two-month sample,
And then we'll know if the plan is ample."
When the audit came back, the Chief's ears were burning,
Since Quon's on-duty texts were full of yearning.
They were hot and spicy; that could not be debated,
And precious few of them were even work-related.

Jeff Quon's fiasco disrupted his life.
He got punished at work and lost his wife.
The sexting and the mistress gave her fits,
So she filed for divorce and called it quits.
Quon's reaction wasn't laid-back or pensive --
He lawyered up and went on the offensive.
He demanded a large recovery
For the Chief's invasion of his privacy.

In federal court, Quon sought a solution
By asserting his rights under the Constitution,
As the Fourth Amendment should protect one
From searches done without a good reason.
The trial and appeals courts could not agree,
So the High Court said, "Alright. We shall see
If a SWAT cop's texts filled with idiocy

Are entitled to the right to privacy."

Court-watchers debated the case in the press:
"What will the nine Justices do with this mess?
Will they set a new policy or will they just bail
On whether bosses must butt out of your texts and email?"

When he came to the courthouse to argue the case,
Quon's mouthpiece got a taste of what they had to face.
After reading the briefs about Quon's deception,
One Justice came up with the following question:
"Do you mean to argue before us and heaven
That a SWAT team cop on-duty 24/7
Should expect his texting on a crime or mutiny
To be immune from public scrutiny?
And if there's a crisis call from nine-one-one
While he's sending a message that's just for fun,
Would the crisis have to wait until he's through
With a voicemail saying 'We'll get back to you'?"

So in the end, what did the Nine decide about Quon's privacy
And what a boss could do to him without committing piracy?
Well, here is what they thought of it and this is how it went:
All Nine agreed that Sergeant Quon should not get one red cent.

Was there a privacy right on the pager -- yea or nay?
The Jurists said: "We'll save that question for another day.
But there is one thing we can all say for certain --
It was legal for the Chief to pull the curtain.
For the workplace we've created a special Fourth Amendment exception
Where a search could be deemed justified at the time of its inception.

If the search is work-related and not for prosecution,
And limited in scope, then we approve of the intrusion."

Sergeant Quon came home from court completely empty-handed;
His win in the appellate court had since been countermanded.
The sordid details of his life became a laughing stock.
So don't assume your texts are safe if you don't want a shock.[11]

Strip Searches in School?

Savanna went to school one day,
But what occurred was no child's play.
In math class at her middle school,
Though she had broken no school rule,
The principal routed her from class
To the school office, where she dared not sass
Officials who when it came to tact
Showed this was something that they lacked.

On the desk a day planner lay open for inspection,
And the principal motioned in its direction.
"Is this yours?" the man demanded to know,
Pointing to contents he wanted to show.
For in the case were things that made him fret:
Some knives, some lighters, and a cigarette.
"Yes, the planner is mine," the girl confessed,
Beginning to feel highly over-stressed,
"But I lent it to a friend days ago,
And those are items that I do not know."

"And what about these?" he asked accusingly,
Laying out three pain pills while glaring meanly.
"I hear you're passing pills around the school,
And you know full well that's breaking a rule."
"Not true!" she replied, "And if you don't believe me,
Then look in my backpack and you will soon see
I have no pills. What's more, I never did,
So I don't know what you heard from some kid."

They searched her backpack, and it proved her right.
There were no pills or contraband in sight.
Then the principal upped the ante --
He had the school nurse search her bra and panty.
The 13-year-old's breasts and genitals were exposed
In the nurse's office when she removed her clothes.
The angst she felt was nearly unbearable --
Her humiliation was just too terrible.

Although in Hollywood nudity is glorified
Displaying her privates left the young girl mortified.
Once again, no pills were discovered, but inside,
The adolescent felt she'd lost more than her pride.

Savanna's Mom filed suit in federal court,
Saying, "Mere belief students hide pills falls short.
They lacked reasonable belief the search would succeed,
Plus, Advil's not dangerous, so there was no need.
The school district is breaking the law with impunity."
But the school district countered: "Well, we've got immunity."

The Supremes considered, in taking their action,
The student's age, sex, and the type of infraction.
For the limited threat posed by common pills for pain relief,
Conducting a strip search of a young girl was beyond belief.
"The strip search," said the Court, "was quite unreasonable.
Under Amendment Four, it's plain indefensible."
Thus, the Court gave Savanna a moral victory
By upholding the teenager's right to privacy,

But beyond that, the Nine could not agree
To side with her Mother financially.
Lower courts had displayed a lot of confusion;
They had not always come to the same conclusion
About strip searches done inside a school,
So there never had been a clear-cut rule.
Thus, the Court held, "We need to grant immunity.
If the law wasn't as clear as it had to be.
We can't punish a governmental entity
If the precedents failed to provide clarity."
It was small consolation to hear they were right
When, for practical purposes, they'd lost the fight.
Savannah and her Mom were quite dejected
When their claim for damages got rejected.[12]

Strip-Searches in Minor Offenses

May motorists be completely divested
Of their clothing upon being arrested?
Does Amendment Four allow a strip-search to commence
Each time one is arrested for a minor offense?
Is that tactic simply over the top
For even the most audacious cop?
Should invasion of one's bodily privacy
Be given the stamp of legitimacy?

What if the search is for the cop's entertainment
And not for legitimate crime containment,
Or is done with the goal of humiliation,
And without grounds for reasonable suspicion?
What sorts of crimes could carry such gravity,
They condone peering into a body cavity?
Could an unbuckled seatbelt or bike with no bell
Subject a person to that kind of hell?
Should marching in an antiwar demonstration
Result in that sort of denigration?

These are questions our Top Court has yet to address,
So we haven't yet learned of potential redress
For grievances due to a cop's undress
Of victims who suffer gratuitous stress.
All we have is the tale of one Albert Florence
Who suffered from angst that was highly intense.

Perhaps he was not the most sterling example
If one could choose from a substantial sample
Of those subjected to a violation
Of privacy without their authorization,
Since once upon a prior occasion,
Albert was charged with flight and evasion
Of police and use of a deadly weapon.
He agreed to pay a fine for his action.
He made payments, but failed to stay abreast,

So a warrant went out for his arrest.
Within a week, he paid up on the case,
But the warrant remained in the database.

Some seven years later, a traffic cop
Saw the warrant and forced his car to stop.
He arrested Albert and took him to county jail,
Where they followed the process for admitting a male.
They peered inside every body cavity.
He felt it affronted his human dignity.
They had him cough while he was crouching,
But at least there was no touching.
They finally released him from that place of terror
Once they learned the arrest was due to their error.

Albert commenced a federal court fight
Over violation of his civil right.
He said those arrested for a minor offense
Should not be subjected to that sort of nonsense
Unless there is good reason to believe
They have guns or drugs somewhere up their sleeve.

The Jurists issued a narrow rule,
Saying, "We believe it's not overly cruel
For an intake process to require such inspection
When one enters a general jail population.
The process won't be deemed too much
If guards are careful not to touch.
The need to ensure jail security
Overrides one's own right to privacy."

However, the Court declined to address
Whether a person might get some redress
In a case where a detainee
Never joins the inmate community,
But remains entirely segregated
Till released on bond or adjudicated.

Four Justices filed this strong dissent:

"It violates the Fourth Amendment
When a person arrested for a minor offense
Not involving drugs or violence
Is given a search that's so invasive --
The entire process is just too repulsive.
A strip-search should be based on reasonable suspicion,
And most courts concur with this proposition."[13]

What It Takes to Win

Shelly Kelly decided to call it quits
With her boyfriend, who was given to fits
Of rage when things didn't go his way --
Shelly feared his reaction on the day
She moved out of her place, to which he had a key.
She asked cops to stand by and secure her safety.

Some officers came who knew of her urgency,
But were soon called away by an emergency.
Then her boyfriend Jerry reared his angry head,
Throwing a temper tantrum when he said,
"I've told you not to call cops on me, bitch!"
Whereupon, he grabbed her and tried to pitch
Her over the railing from the second floor.
She got what she'd expected, and a whole lot more.

She feared for her life, and fled to her car.
Yet, that didn't get her very far,
Since he grabbed his shotgun and threatened to shoot
If she tried to leave. But that issue was moot.
She floored the pedal, and off she sped,
Driving her vehicle, full speed ahead.
Jerry fired five shots at her as she fled.
The shots hit a tire, but missed her head.
She managed to escape, fairly intact
Because she had been so quick to react.

Kelly phoned the police to report the assault.
They felt bad, since it might have been partly their fault.
She mentioned that Jerry belonged to the Crips --
Cops could do a lot with those sorts of tips.
The thought of a street gang caught their attention
More than anything else that she could mention.

A detective opened an investigation,
And Kelly helped to provide information.
When asked where Jerry lived, Kelly confided,

His foster mom's home was where he resided.
The cop found his rap sheet -- umpteen pages in all.
There were thirty-one crimes where he'd taken a fall.

The detective looked for a way to pry
Any guns out of the hands of that guy.
When seeking a warrant to find something wrong,
His wish list of items was awfully long.
So when he submitted his application,
It looked much like a gang investigation.
Besides listing every gun in creation,
He included proof of gang affiliation.
A judge thought the paperwork looked OK,
And approved the warrant that very day.

When a team of cops forced open her door,
The foster mom felt she could stand it no more.
Ms. Millender, her daughter and grandson
Were jolted when police grabbed her shotgun.
Two weeks later, cops found Jerry in a motel,
And transported him straight to a local jail cell.

But the incident spawned a great deal of ill will,
And the Millender family would not sit still.
They sued the cops and County of L.A.
For invading their home on that fateful day,
Saying the warrant had been far too broad.
Ergo, it was constitutionally flawed.
The judge found the lawsuit could not be negated
Unless Jerry's actions were gang-related.
What's more, the cops could not claim immunity --
Probable cause is required in the legal community.

Was the warrant tailored by probable cause
To think Jerry had broken specific laws?
Was he angry becuz
Kelly called the fuzz,
Or was he aggrieved
That she wanted to leave?

Did his crime arise out of domestic strife,
Or his fear she'd tell cops of his gangster's life?

The Supremes agreed to explain how they saw
The test for when cops pay for breaking the law.
"Police cannot escape liability
Where judges shirk their responsibility.
But when the judge's mistake is so great
That *all* reasonable cops would appreciate
The fact that the warrant lacked probable cause,
We'll hold cops to account for breaking the laws.
If the cops' incompetence is not clear and plain,
We won't subject them to that kind of pain.
So we're letting these officers off the hook,
Since their actions came close enough to the book."

The dissent complained, "Every Founding Father
Would object to this use of unbridled power.
Police should be held to articulate
The items they need, and show how they relate
To a specific, well-defined crime.
Our decisions must stand the test of time.
We should penalize a fishing expedition,
Since the law bans police from that sort of mission.
What we've done encourages cops to neglect
The very rights they are sworn to protect."[14]

Chapter IV. Representation, Self-Incrimination, and Identification

Fifth Amendment: No person ... shall be compelled in any criminal case to be a witness against himself....

Sixth Amendment: In all criminal prosecutions, the accused shall enjoy the right to a speedy and public trial, by an impartial jury ... to be confronted with the witnesses against him ... and to have the Assistance of Counsel for his defence.

Fourteenth Amendment: ... No State shall make or enforce any law which shall abridge the privileges or immunities of citizens of the United States, nor shall any State deprive any person of life, liberty, or property, without due process of law; nor deny to any person within its jurisdiction the equal protection of the laws.

Gideon's Gamble

In nineteen sixty-one, a man of no report
Sent a handwritten plea to the U.S. High Court.
The odds were stacked against him when he filed his plea,
But the stakes could not be higher -- his liberty.
While he'd never advanced past the eighth grade in school,
Clarence Earl Gideon was nobody's fool.
Though pegged as a gambler and a petty thief,
In this case he had a legitimate beef.

He went on trial for burglary,
A crime classed as a felony.
He had good reason to resent
That charge, since he was innocent.

He told the judge, "I'm not ready to be tried --
Unless I get a lawyer my hands are tied.
I have no money to hire an attorney,
So I'm asking you to appoint one for me."

Alas -- the law in Florida, where he faced doing time,
Said you only get free counsel for a *capital* crime.
He argued his case, but while he did his best,
His oratory was not up to the test,
Since he lacked the skill to dampen the fury
Of that six-man Florida state court jury.
He knew not how to make those jurors see
He wouldn't need to break in -- he had a key
To the pool hall where he was an employee.
That unjust trial would go down in infamy.
The man who told cops that Gideon broke in
Had fingered Gideon to save his own skin.

When he lost his case and got sent to jail,
He reached out to the Court by U.S. mail.
His petition voiced this simple plea:

"Due process was denied to me.
I asked the judge for counsel. He refused this aid,
But that goes against a ruling your Court made.[1]
The Fourteenth Amendment has indicated
That due process of law is violated
When a poor man suffers from a denial
Of counsel for his felony trial."

But the High Court had held, in an old report,
"That rule applies only in federal court."[2]
The Supremes, in old cases he did not know,
Had held folks in state courts would have to show
Compelling reasons for being anointed
With the privilege of having counsel appointed,
Like youth, illiteracy, mental illness,
Special circumstances, or basic unfairness.
For Gideon, things were not looking good,
Since for two decades, that's how the law stood.
Unbeknownst to him, the papers he signed
Asked the U.S. High Court to change its mind.[3]

When his plea reached the Court, it drew little attention.
But that changed when a gent of honorable mention,
A partner at a D.C. firm of great distinction,
Agreed to champion the pauper's petition.
At Yale Law School, Abe Fortas made his debut
As Editor-in-Chief of the law review.
As a cabinet member for F.D.R.,
He'd proven to be a fast-rising star.
As an advocate, he'd launched a reform once before.
His career was studded with achievements galore.

The billable hours Fortas and his firm poured
Into the case topped what most folks could afford.
He learned Florida's top court was a repeat offender --
Four times, it got reversed for lack of a public defender.
He found the Sunshine State trailed most of the rest --
For free counsel, most used a more generous test.
Part of his task -- to convince the High Court

Costs wouldn't leave counties on life-support.

Florida's A.G. reached out from his corner
To all U.S. states, seeking to garner
Reinforcement by *amicus curiae*[4]
To argue the Court's same ole rules should lie.
But much to the Florida A.G.'s surprise,
Twenty-three states argued contrariwise.
They called the old case law outmoded and curious,
And the "special circumstances rule," spurious.
They urged Gideon's conviction be set aside.
Just two states chimed in to prop up Florida's side.
Opposition to that state's stance is no mystery --
Its pared-down law stood on the wrong side of history.

At oral argument, the A.G. had to admit
Some folks tried without counsel were illiterate.
Abe Fortas, *au contraire*, did just fine.
His argument won over all Nine.

A unanimous Court found the old rules *passé* --
Future trials must be conducted in a new way:
"The right to counsel is so fundamental
To fair trials, it's plainly elemental.
The Fourteenth Amendment mandates no less
Than lawyers on *both* sides for due process."

Defying inertia and fear of state power,
Gideon had stubbornly refused to cower.
That humble soul's plea spawned a case so iconic,
It led to a shift nothing short of tectonic.
Lawyers in state courts to fight the good fight
On behalf of the poor, mushroomed overnight.
Gideon got a lawyer and a new trial,
Where despite his accuser's defiant denial,
Jurors thought the accuser committed the crime,
And Gideon's gamble paid off big time.[5]

Lawyers Keep Out

The story we tell is a very sad story,
Where none but the lawyer is covered in glory.
Grace lived with her spouse in a Windy City flat,
Where he beat her whenever they had a spat.
One frigid night, as he entered the door,
Her husband collapsed and fell flat on the floor.
Cops found he'd been shot in the back of the head --
Her hard-hearted spouse was decidedly dead.

Cops had little to go on, save their suspicion,
So finding the culprit became their mission.
They nabbed Grace's brother in a warrantless arrest,
And took him downtown to put him to the test.
But he hired a lawyer who said, "Just stay mum."
When they tried to ask questions, Danny played dumb.
The next event shows how much can be gained
By quick access to counsel you have retained.
Counsel got a court order. Cops could not make him stay,
And they had to spring Danny later that day.

Ten days passed with no progress to show
Till cops nabbed a man named DiGerlando.
Police sat him down, handcuffed to a chair,
Then kicked the chair over and left him there.
Four cops beat the man and squeezed all his privates
Over a time span of twenty minutes.
They struck him on the neck, the ribs and the chest
To convince him confessing would be best.
They gave him no food or water to drink --
One gets better treatment in the clink.
He finally confessed Grace hired him to kill
Her husband for five hundred-dollar bills.
He told them two others were in on the plan --
Danny Escobedo and one other man.

That night cops hauled in both Danny and Grace,

Determined to question them face-to-face.
Danny was placed in a tricky situation
Due to what transpired at his interrogation.
Danny kept asking to talk to his lawyer,
Who was cooling his heels at police headquarters.
Despite his demand to see Danny at the station,
They said, "Not till we finish the interrogation."
Though he showed cops the law said he could see his client,
He left at one a.m., since they were not compliant.
While trying to see Danny, counsel had no clue
That police told Danny, "He declines to see you."

The cops figured any lawyer worth his salt
Would bring the questioning to a screeching halt,
And they didn't want counsel to put a stop
To the game they were playing -- good cop, bad cop.
Danny, a young man of Mexican extraction
Was handcuffed in a standing position
When an officer who knew Danny's family
Spoke Spanish to Danny, and seemed very friendly.
"I want to help you so you don't go down.
You can leave if you pin the blame on that clown.
DiGerlando said you're the one who shot
Your brother-in-law. Is that true or not?"
Danny replied, "The answer is no."
The cop urged, "Why don't you tell him so?"

Cops brought them together, and for the first time,
Danny conceded he knew of the crime.
By telling his friend, "*You* fired the shot,"
He implicated himself in the plot.
Cops did not explain that Danny's complicity
Made him guilty due to accountability.
They procured the admission by playing on his fear
That silence would not be an option -- that was clear.
They conceded he wasn't told of his right
To stay quiet during the grilling that night.

The statement obtained during custody
Got used at his trial successfully.
But counsel argued that allowing the statement
Breached Danny's rights under the Sixth Amendment,
Since Danny's right to counsel had been denied
When he asked for his lawyer, but was deprived.

The lower courts held to the contrary,
Saying, "Danny's confession was voluntary,
And lack of counsel in interrogation
Has never been deemed a violation.
Police may be midwife to a declaration
Born of remorse, desperation, or calculation.
There's a natural compulsion to confess,
So Danny Escobedo has no redress."
But the High Court agreed to take a look
And see if the cops had played by the book.

Danny's case spawned a High Court revolution,
Since those Jurists invoked the Constitution
To change the process for interrogation
At police departments throughout the nation.
They said, "Interrogation's a 'critical stage'
Where the guiding hand of counsel could presage
The outcome. If access to counsel had to follow
Questioning, the right to counsel would be hollow.
The right to counsel enshrined in the Sixth Amendment
Forbids use of an incriminating statement
Secured from a suspect in police custody
When they bar him from meeting with his attorney."[6]

D.A.s to Keep Mum about Silence

When Griffin failed to testify at his trial,
The D.A. made much of his lack of denial.
In giving his closing to the jury,
He whipped them into a red-hot fury.
He told them a rather lurid story
With facts that were both gruesome and gory.
He said, "Griffin would know why Ellie Mae
Appeared so beaten up when he walked away.
He declines to take the stand and explain
Why he left Ellie Mae in so much pain."

It was up to the jury to rule yea or nay.
They put great stock in what the D.A. had to say.
The jury found Griffin to be guilty,
And imposed the ultimate penalty.

Did it violate the Fifth Amendment
For the D.A. to utter that comment?
Is a no-comment rule needed to protect
The right to keep quiet and give it respect?

The High Court later waded into the fray
To decide if a "comment rule" is OK.
Said the Court, "It deserves condemnation
As a remnant of the Inquisition.
It condones imposing a penalty
On a right by making it too costly.
Since the Fifth Amendment applies to the states,
There should be no remaining rule that negates
The exercise of a Fifth Amendment right.
So it's time to bid that old rule goodnight.
D.A.s and trial judges must not succumb
To faulting defendants for staying mum,
And must avoid any insinuation
That taking the Fifth should lead to conviction."[7]

Miranda

Miranda is a name that most school kids would know,
Since cops give the warnings on each TV cop show.
The mantra they quote is no longer a novelty --
The warnings are part of our cultural history.
Today, police find them so indispensable,
Doing without them seems incomprehensible.

Our Fifth Amendment stems from protests seeking abolition
Of ancient English practices much like an inquisition.
American colonists had the foresight to worry
Lest America fall prey to that sort of inquiry.
They vowed that they'd never allow a Star Chamber
Where folks were compelled to come up with an answer.
They wanted a system that would guarantee
Silence as a right, with speech not compulsory.

In nineteen sixty-six, the Court found it apropos
To set concrete guidelines for police to follow.
The Jurists sought to impose a limitation
On rampant abuses in interrogation.
Their consternation appeared to flow
From misconduct seen in *Escobedo*.[6]
Their goal -- to protect from police trickery
All suspects taken into custody.
For even without police brutality,
Innocents may succumb to the third degree.

When Miranda's case came to their attention,
Here's how the Justices framed the question:
"Where a confession is technically 'voluntary,'
We need to decide if warnings are necessary
To overcome the inherent compulsion
Of custodial settings rife with coercion.
We must guard the right against self-incrimination,
Since it's one of the principal rights in our nation."

A parade of horrors the Court recounted
That in the past, police had mounted
To pressure those who, when met with deception,
Would confess if fed an undue suggestion.
Once alone with a subject, police might persist
In undermining one's will to resist,
Until the cop's persistent obsession
Eventually led to a false confession.
While in custody, one is incommunicado,
And susceptible to threats and bravado.
The third degree, scholars say, is the lazy man's way,
While cops who pound the pavement earn their pay.
A real search for the truth is not so uncouth
As a twelve-hour grilling of an uninformed youth.

Justice Warren spoke on behalf of the Court:
"Sadly, today's police practices fall short --
Some confessions come from use of brutality,
But more often, there's a new reality.
Our solution is aimed at curtailing a ritual
That you'll find prescribed in a standard police manual,
Where cops are taught to use psychology
As the hallmark of their strategy.
They're trained to play good cop, bad cop,
To place the suspect in a rigged line-up,
Or offer the person false legal advice
To deter him from claiming his Constitutional right."

The Court spelled out four warnings that cops must impart.
At the time, it seemed like a good place to start.
The warnings were no doubt a sterling idea,
But fall somewhat short of a panacea.
So here are the warnings, with a few oblique
Comments about that mandated technique:

"You have the right to remain silent." [A good thing to know.]

"Anything you say may be used against you." [A fair *quid pro quo*.]
"You can have counsel present during questioning." [Doesn't say how.]
"If you can't afford a lawyer, the court will appoint one." [But not right now!]

The Court laid down this ruling: "In a criminal prosecution,
D.A.s may not use statements from a custodial interrogation
Unless the suspect is first warned by the State
That he's not required to cooperate.
If the suspect chooses silence, it's incumbent on police
That interrogation be foregone and immediately cease.
When we say he must be 'in custody,'
We mean this applies to those who aren't free
To leave the room and go on their way
Instead of feeling compelled to stay.

"This decision creates an 'Exclusionary Rule'
Banning un-Mirandized statements as a D.A.'s tool.
The warnings are geared to be prophylactic
By guarding against a coercive cop's tactic.
But the warnings are also squarely meant
To implement the Fifth Amendment."

In dissent, a vocal four-Justice minority
Declared, "We think there's a gaping paucity
Of experience drawn from the past
To show the new rules aren't too much too fast.
So many new rules should make the Court choke.
Why fix the system if it ain't broke?"[8]

Speak up to Remain Silent

The Warren Court promulgated an idea,
Later rejected by Roberts and Scalia,
Who with Kennedy, Thomas and Alito
Were quite eager to see some restrictions go.
Warren tried to defuse a cop's obsession
That could sometimes lead to a false confession
When the law lets cops use *sub rosa* strategy
While questioning suspects detained in custody.

Over forty years after *Miranda* became law,
A new Court majority figured they saw
A way to erode the protections given
When the old guard's majority seemed so driven.

A shooting outside a shopping mall
Led to Van Chester Thompkins taking a fall.
Two cops placed him in a room that was very small,
Where they gave him a copy of his rights and all.
They checked to make sure he knew how to read,
And figured that was all they would need
To make sure that Thompkins understood,
And asked him to sign it so all would be good.
But Thompkins refused to sign the form,
Despite their urging that he perform.

Since he never said, "No," the cops thought they could go
Ahead and ask questions to see what he might know.
Yet, for nearly three hours he sat without talking
While cops kept posing questions without balking.
For most of that time, Thompkins kept up his guard,
Except when he told them his chair was too hard.
But toward the end, one cop said something odd --
He asked Thompkins if he believed in God.
Thompkins said, "Yes." All at once, his eyes
Filled with tears, much to the cop's surprise.
"Do you pray to God?" the officer said.

To which Thompkins said "Yes" and nodded his head.
"Did you seek forgiveness for shooting that boy down?",
The cop asked. Then Thompkins said "Yes," making a
frown.

Although Thompkins declined to sign any paper
Confessing, the D.A. charged him with murder.
At trial, defense counsel said that the cop,
Under *Miranda*, was required to stop
The questioning once Thompkins demonstrated denial,
So his statements should not be allowed at trial.
But the judge turned down counsel's motion to suppress,
And the statements came in, much to his distress.
The defendant got life without parole
To pay for the life he allegedly stole.

The case wound up before the Roberts Court.
Five of nine Jurists issued this report:
"The fact that Thompkins never spoke
During questioning failed to invoke
His Fifth Amendment right to cease
Interrogation by police.
Defendant was required to say
He would not talk to cops that day,
Since otherwise they could not know
They had to stop and not to go.
While it's true the *Miranda* decision said
You can't presume their rights have been forfeited,
When suspects refrain from communication
Or later break down in a confession,
We've come up with a more sensible rule.
So from now on, the cops will have a new tool.
The burden's on suspects to invoke their rights.
This rule should prevent future courtroom fights."

Justice Sotomayor wrote for the four
Justices who seemed to cringe in horror
At the notion that a suspect's required to speak
To guard his right to silence. That aroused their pique.

She spoke on behalf of all four when she said, "This case turns the *Miranda* rule on its head."[9]

YOUR RIGHTS WHEN STOPPED BY POLICE   Nancy E. Albert

Not So Mum Anymore

Two brothers in their Houston flat got shot,
But the trail went cold before it turned hot.
A neighbor saw a Trans Am leave the scene,
Yet other clues were few and far between.
One telltale clue the shooter left behind --
Some shotgun shells -- a very lucky find!
Cops spoke with tenants in the housing complex,
But failed to get a lead on any suspects.

Weeks later, someone fed the cops a good lead --
Salinas had a shotgun -- did he do the deed?
Eventually, cops came to the door
Of his parents' house, and said what they'd come for.
When cops saw a Trans Am in the driveway,
They sensed a break might come their way that day.
Cops had no warrant with them when them came --
They only had an address and a name.

The folks agreed to let them look around,
And when cops searched the home, a shotgun was found.
Said the cops, "We'd like to talk to your son;
Perhaps he can help to nab the right one."
They said their goal was just investigation,
So Salinas agreed to come to the station.

At the station, cops put him in an interview room
And peppered him with questions. The place felt like a tomb.
Miranda warnings were never delivered.
Salinas simply stayed put and quivered.
Cops said they could clear him as a suspect,
So he played along and failed to object.
But it's hard to believe
That he felt free to leave.

He answered questions till they posed a hard one --

Would the shells from the scene be a match for his gun?
He then fell silent, as was his right,
Though *Miranda* warnings cops had failed recite.
The cops thought Salinas's pregnant pause
Was more than enough to give them some cause
To suspect the man of murder, though they never told him so.
But the D.A. said they had no proof, and had to let him go.

Then out of the blue, cops got a windfall --
Salinas's friend volunteered it all:
Salinas spoke to him and spilled the beans --
He'd made the hit, with his shotgun as the means.

At his murder trial, Salinas never spoke,
So the D.A. could not cross-examine the bloke.
A ballistics report found the shells from the scene
Seemed to match the suspect's gun's magazine.
But the D.A. could not present proof positive --
He needed more to make his case dispositive.

With the cop on the stand,
The D.A. took command:
"Regarding the shell casings, did he refute
Your theory?" "No," said the cop. "Salinas stood mute,
Then he looked at the floor, bit his lip,
Shuffled his feet, and tightened up.
From his body language, it was plain to see
The man's as guilty as Simon Legree."
Said the D.A., "We've sewn up this patchwork quilt --
Salinas's silence is proof of his guilt."

When the jury learned of the suspect's silence,
They found him guilty, and for his sentence,
The court meted out a punishment
Of twenty years' imprisonment.

The Texas appeals courts had never opined

On whether non-custodial silence could be mined
For use against those who'd not testified.
Shouldn't the D.A.'s hands have been tied?
Should the privilege not to speak have been triggered?
In this case did Amendment Five get rejiggered?
Federal appeals courts were split on the question,
So the Bench took it on at defendant's suggestion.

Here's how the Court framed the question on appeal:
If a target opts for silence and declines to squeal,
Could the un-Mirandized pre-arrest target invoke
His right to silence if he never spoke?
To claim the Fifth what did he need to do?
Could he just clam up or say, "To heck with you"?

The lawyers launched into a lively debate.
Whose view would the Court more appreciate?
To the D.A., the warnings weren't necessary,
Since Salinas was never "in custody."
He was free to leave, and the talks were friendly,
So the suspect's acts should be deemed "voluntary."

The defense said, "There's but one conclusion to draw:
Commenting on the suspect's silence broke the law.
Plus, cops reeled in the suspect by using a ruse --
Should the courts egg them on when they seek to confuse?"

The Bench knew this to be a sticky wicket,
But nonetheless they charged into the thicket.
Despite their work, they could not muster more
Than a split in opinions of three-two-four.
Three right-wing Jurists found the suspect lost his fight
To claim the Fifth by not invoking it outright.
They defaulted to a phrase that sounded highfalutin --
"The self-incrimination right's not self-executin'."

Two others said the trio dodged the main question:
Should the D.A. in closing be allowed to mention

That a suspect while not in custody refused to speak,
And then to use his silence in critique?
To this, the duo answered, "Yes he can --
His comments fall outside the Fifth's ban.
Amendment Five has nothing to say
On that topic, and thus holds no sway."
Thus, three plus two came out on the same side
By agreeing to let the conviction ride.

Four dissenters said, "Both conclusions are absurd.
How could a suspect come up with the right word
To invoke his right to silence when he was never told
That words were something he could rightfully withhold?
In such a case, how could the Court place blame
On failing to mention the Fifth by name?
The plurality offers a Hobson's choice --
If you don't speak, you'll still have used your voice."[10]

Miranda for Kids

A seventh grade student in special ed
Learned something he hadn't anticipated.
He attended his social studies class,
But found himself mired in a murky morass
When an officer barged into his classroom,
Then marched him to a room he was apt to assume
Was not a place from which he could break free,
And two cops then gave him the third degree.
They closed the door, and questioned away,
But never told him, "You don't have to stay."
Nor did they warn him, "You're free to decline
To answer our questions. That would be fine."
They made it clear that, if he failed to confess
To some break-ins of homes, he'd be in a mess.
Then one of the cops proceeded to mention
That he could get sent to juvenile detention
If he did not provide a complete report --
That had to be done *before* going to court.

When he heard the words, "juvenile detention,"
The 13-year-old snapped to attention.
The threat made him eager to agree
To accept responsibility.
Once the cop secured the confession,
He made the following concession:
"You don't have to answer another question,
And you're free to leave at your discretion."
But before he left, the highly distressed
Boy signed a statement at the cop's request.

The boy, whose initials were J.D.B.,
Got charged with larceny and B and E.
The boy's public defender moved to exclude
The statement, and argued with certitude
That cops withheld warnings illegally
While keeping the boy in their custody.
But the trial judge said, "I do not agree;

I find him guilty of delinquency."

On review, the Nine undertook to gauge
The relevance of a young person's age.
Would a youth have concluded he could scoff
At the questioning and then simply bug off?
"A child's age is more than a fact,"
Said the Court. "It affects how they act.
Children lack perspective about their choices,
And are vulnerable to adult voices.
Events that would not make a grown man feel bad
Could have a dramatic effect on a lad.
So long as the cops know about the child's age,
They need to consider that when they engage
The youth to judge whether his frailty
Means he should be viewed as 'in custody,'
And therefore entitled to get a warning,
And a chance to say no to the questioning."

The dissent said, "While this ruling sounds sensible,
To cops, it might be too incomprehensible,
For even in cases where they have an inkling
About a kid's age, they would need to do thinking.
We prefer a rule that's one-size-fits-all.
Miranda's set up to be a cop's call."[11]

Gideon Redux

Post-*Gideon*, the law remained somewhat in doubt,
Since the Court had refrained from explaining flat out --
Does a poor man's right to counsel stop at the door
Of a felony charge, or encompass much more?
It took most of a decade, as cases came and went,
For a candidate to show up and clearly present
The question the Jurists had long waited for --
Would there need to be public defenders galore?
The case found its way from the Sunshine State.
Like *Gideon*, it arrived rather late.

The charge in this cause may seem out of date --
A concealed weapon made the man jailbait.
That was long before laws said most everyone
Could walk around packing a hidden gun.
The state's law called it a "petty offense,"
With a fine or brief jail stay as recompense.
The most they could give, for a crime they called petty,
Would be six months inside a reformatory.
The trial judge forged ahead, nor did he linger
Before meting out jail time to Jon Argersinger.

In seeking redress, the pauper had to resort
To a habeas action in the state's high court.
He charged that at his lower court trial
The judge had persisted in denial
Of his right to counsel, so he couldn't present
His defense or make a good legal argument.
The state's high court became anxious and pensive,
Saying, "What you're asking would be too expensive.
Where a person's not risking a long penalty,
He's not entitled to a lawyer for free."

Jon's habeas case made one final stop --
He took his plea all the way to the top.
As we said, the Supremes were lying in wait
For the wheels of justice to grind toward that date.

They entered the fray with full recognition
That this was a problem of huge dimension,
Since the number of court cases, they were told,
Requiring free counsel could increase tenfold.

They took up the task that was left undone,
And when the Nine voted, they spoke as one.
"We're not convinced it's any simpler to present
A defense where a petty charge leads to imprisonment.
Counsel's needed any time one will be
Deprived of his life or his liberty.

"America's courts have acquired an obsession
With rushing cases to a quick disposition.
Courts tend to see dockets as numbers to process,
Not people who suffer from problems and great stress.
Those charged with small crimes get assembly-line justice
Where denial of counsel leads to prejudice.
Studies show, when defendants have an attorney,
Dismissal of charges is five times more likely.
Courts rely too much on the guilty plea
And too little on treating the accused fairly.

"To the jaded, a short sentence might seem of no moment,
But the prospect of jail time is a life-changing event.
That our legal system should be fair and just
Is not a choice -- it's an absolute must.
So no one may be jailed for any offense
Without first having counsel for his defense."[12]

Are Lawyers for the Poor up to Par?

About two decades after Gideon's case,
The Court decided it's the right time and place
To lay down some standards by which to decide
When a lawyer's performance is just too cockeyed.

So what does the right-to-counsel mean?
What if the lawyer is unskilled and green?
Is having a law degree good enough,
Or does counsel need to have the right stuff?[13]

David Leroy Washington
Was not the finest specimen
For a case to test the potential right
Of the poor to lawyers who are topflight.
A church-going man, he proved rather sinister
In the wake of his stabbing of a minister.
He went on a ten-day-long crime spree,
Robbing, torturing and killing with glee.
His victims were black, white, young and old,
And all of his murders were heartless and cold.
He offed three strangers in a manner quite gruesome,
So his scruples ranked somewhat lower than pond scum.
Hence, he failed to garner much empathy
When claiming his sentence was a travesty.

The trial court appointed counsel for his defense,
And counsel gave his client advice that made sense.
He pursued pretrial motions and discovery,
But his work came to naught when Dave grew ornery.
He completely ignored counsel's sound advice
By waiving a jury and admitting guilt thrice.
He then waived his right to a sentencing jury,
Expecting the trial judge to show sympathy
When he accepted responsibility
For killing three people quite brutally.
The judge reacted to his cruelty
By sentencing him to the death penalty.

He argued his lawyer could have done more
At the sentencing phase to even the score
By calling some friends to testify
That he was a really kind and nice guy,
And by seeking to show that he's mentally ill,
Though the evidence of that was nil.

Said the High Court, "We need to devise a test
For when, due to inadequate counsel, it's best
To reverse the outcome of a criminal judgment
For running afoul of the Sixth Amendment.
The Sixth Amendment has no guarantee
That assistance rendered be top quality.
Rather, its role is to prevent denial
Of a just and fundamentally fair trial.
We won't reverse a conviction or sentence
Unless the defense can show two components:
The lawyer's work was of such poor quality
That it fell below norms of the legal community,
And the deficient performance was so remiss,
The defense case suffered 'prejudice.'
Prejudice means there's a probability
That things would have turned out differently
If counsel had done the job properly.
This defendant has made no showing
That unreliability or prejudice was flowing
From the sentence the trial court judge imposed,
Or counsel's failings when the judge said, 'Case closed'."

Justice Marshall wrote a scathing dissent
On the meaning of the Sixth Amendment.
"It's sad that those who can pay counsel's fee
Need not settle like those in poverty.
We abdicate judicial responsibility
By setting a standard of such ambiguity.
The Court is allowing uncertainty to smolder,
Since deciphering its standard's in the eye of the beholder.
As for the Court's second prong,

The need to show prejudice is all wrong.
Once a case is botched, it's really too late --
To tell what could've been, you'd have to speculate."[14]

Horse Trading

Gideon's case may bring on a smile,
Since once he got a lawyer for his trial,
His attorney helped the jury to see
That another man did the burglary.
After all, in a country that's fair and free,
Isn't that how a trial is supposed to be?

O.J.'s lawyer argued, "You must acquit"
When he showed the jury the glove didn't fit.
A media circus infected the trial.
For O.J., his lawyers proved very worthwhile.

Casey Anthony's lawyer blamed her parents
For her sweet little daughter's disappearance.
His theatrics got the Tot Mom acquitted,
Though they left doubts about what she'd committed.

But trials like the public sees on TV
Are in fact a relative rarity.
Few cases garner the sound and fury
Of counsel's antics before a jury.
In the U.S., there can be no denial
That few criminal cases go to trial.
The average is around five per cent.
In our system, that hardly makes a dent.
The rest are resolved, there's no debating
By a form of modern-day horse trading.
This practice puts pressure on the innocent to plead,
While for the guilty, a reduced sentence is guaranteed.

If there is no trial, with all its whoop-de-do,
Then what's the defense lawyer required to do?
Said the Court, "Plea bargaining is an art,
And lawyers are obliged to do their part.
Plea bargaining is not an aberration --
It's how the justice system works in our nation.
We can't ignore the simple reality

That guilty pleas grease the system's machinery.
Due to the vast quantities of cases
Our criminal justice system faces
We need plea bargaining as a default,
Lest the system grind to a screeching halt."

The High Court reviewed the role of the attorney
In two cases where each took a different journey.
In one case, defense counsel failed to convey
An offer that expired on a certain day.
The client much later copped a plea
On terms far less satisfactory.

In the second, counsel said to reject the deal
Where they should have grabbed it, since it was a real steal.
The accused went to trial; the outcome was horrible --
The man's sentence proved to be quite astronomical.

The Court ruled that, "Defense lawyers owe a duty
To convey formal plea offers very promptly,
And failure to do so in this instance
Amounts to ineffective assistance.
This failure is such a blatant omission,
We find it's at odds with the Constitution.
Defendants need adequate representation
At this 'critical stage' of the prosecution."

As for counsel who gave the dreadful advice
That led to the trial where they rolled the dice,
The Court held his performance fell well below
The standard of competence lawyers should know.

Scalia wrote, for both cases, dissents,
And put in his forthright unvarnished two cents:
"The plea bargaining system is like a casino.
It really belongs in Las Vegas and Reno.
At best, it's an unavoidable evil --
Perhaps the device is the work of the devil.

"The criminal process has grown far too long,
And the Court's approach to it has been all wrong.
We've managed to burden the criminal process
In the fruitless pursuit of too-perfect justice.

"The Court today opens a whole new field --
Plea-bargaining standards are now revealed.
We've invented a right to effective plea bargaining.
Mark my words -- one day we'll regret this opening.
We've gone and built a sparkling new edifice,
An outcome-based test for finding prejudice.
This horse trading calls for some sort of solution,
But who says that's the job of the Constitution?"[15]

Vonlee and Her Guilty Plea

A transgender woman by the name of Vonlee
Learned that not every wrong has a remedy.
Her first lawyer arranged for a rather fair plea
That she'd get in exchange for her testimony
Against her Aunt Billie, who'd offed Billie's spouse --
The man had a rep as a well-to-do souse.

Billie and Vonlee shared a rather odd story,
Somewhat bizarre, though not overly gory.
The aunt offered her niece a tidy sum
If she'd help kill her spouse and then stay mum.
On the date in question, they came in the back door,
And found Billie's spouse passed out on the floor.
Billie came up with a ghoulish plan
To pour vodka down the throat of the man
While closing the airway from his nose
As he remained in a state of repose.
At first, Vonlee helped, but then she relented.
She got Billie to halt the scheme she'd invented.
But once Vonlee walked away from that space,
Billie stuck a pillow over his face,
And that was the end of the hard-drinking man
Who died in his kitchen beside the trash can.

Vonlee tried to stay mum, but couldn't stop --
She told her lover, who then told a cop.
The women were charged with murder one,
And soon the plea bargaining had begun.
The State offered Vonlee 7-to-15
If she'd testify to the events she'd seen.

The deal appeared to be all cut-and-dried
Till Vonlee passed a test to see if she'd lied.
She then told a jailer she shouldn't do time,
Since she really had nothing to do with the crime.
The jailer helped her to hire someone new
Who'd make sure Vonlee's case would get a redo.

The new lawyer rushed to withdraw her plea
Without doing his homework so he could see
All the evidence stacked up against Vonlee
That was massive and incriminatory.
He told the D.A. she'd refuse to squeal
Unless he would cut her a better deal.
When the D.A. replied, "Decidedly no,"
He bailed out of the case with nothing to show.

Court-appointed counsel took the case to trial,
Where Vonlee told the truth, and made no denial
Regarding her role in that home-brewed stew.
The jury found her guilty of murder two.
Said the judge, "You won't be allowed to go free
Till you serve your new sentence: 20-to-40."

The matter found its way to the Top Court,
Where the Justices gave this brief retort:
"Amendment Six can't assure perfection --
It all boils down to a simple question:
Did Vonlee receive adequate advice
Before making the choice to roll the dice?
While it's true, counsel failed to study the case
Before he let things blow up in his face,
And his role in withdrawing Vonlee's plea
Fell far short of being exemplary,
There's nothing wrong with withdrawing a plea
Where a suspect proclaims she's not guilty.

"It's not our job to second-guess
Work done by a state court to assess
Defense counsel's effectiveness.
Vonlee has received her due process."[16]

Should We Second-Guess an Eyewitness?

Eyewitnesses can provide the key
To solving an inscrutable mystery.
But what is the best way to I.D.
The perps when cops lack their identity?

In a line-up, a show-up, or photo array,
There are perils all along the way.
What if the witness sees the suspect before
Stepping into the line-up, in cuffs at the door?
What of a line where one guy's six feet tall,
And three others are extremely small?
Or there could be a problematic show-up,
Where a lone suspect is seen next to a cop.

Can a shaken witness
Who's beset by distress
When caught up in a mess
Recall the perp's mode of dress,
Or his face, height and shape
As he made his escape?

How can courts ensure the reliability
Of I.D.s rife with suggestibility,
And avoid unfair influence on a jury,
Resulting in irreparable injury?

In the sixties, the Court excluded identification
When obtained by employing a suggestive
confrontation.
But over time, the Court eroded that rule,
And rarely approved that Draconian tool.
Instead, the Court said you could use an I.D.
That meets these tests of reliability:
Did he get a good look
At that dastardly crook,
And for how long a time
Did he view the crime?

Did he pay close attention
To the perp's description?
Was he really, truly sure,
Or is his memory poor?
How long had it been
Since they had the run-in?[17]

Then in two thousand twelve, the Court added one more
Hurdle for the defense that could change the score.
Said the Court, "Since our aim is to keep cops from rigging
The I.D. procedures, we've had to keep digging.
So we've come up with a new way to decide
When it's okay for courts to let the I.D. ride:
Even if the suggestive I.D. enhances
The D.A.'s case, if the circumstances
Were not arranged by the authorities,
They can use it as if it had bona fides."

Justice Sotomayor filed the sole dissent,
Contesting the majority's argument.
"No matter who arranges the deception,
Such I.D.s impact a juror's perception.
In the end, it can lead to an unfair trial,
And often result in the denial
Of due process required by the Constitution.
The Court's new rule is a bad solution.
It reduces the trial to a mere formality
Lacking reliability and credibility.
For the past thirty years, every study has shown
That suggestive I.D.s are very prone
To result in a wrongful conviction
Based on a misidentification.
The dangers at trial of undue suggestion
Deserve more careful consideration."[18]

Chapter V. Taking Aim at Gun Laws

Second Amendment: A well-regulated militia, being necessary to the security of a free State, the right of the people to keep and bear Arms, shall not be infringed.

Fourteenth Amendment: ... No State shall make or enforce any law which shall abridge the privileges or immunities of citizens of the United States, nor shall any State deprive any person of life, liberty, or property, without due process of law; nor deny to any person within its jurisdiction the equal protection of the laws.

Guns and the Constitution

The Second Amendment has sparked and ignited
Debates that get so many people excited.
Although the whole thing is just one sentence long,
Everybody thinks someone else has it wrong.
In the first clause, it is stipulated
That militias must be regulated
For the security of a free state.
That is the whole of the clause's mandate.
The second says, "the people" have a right
To bear arms, but those words have caused a fight,
Since some think they're just about arms meant for war.
Others say self-defense is what they're meant for.
Could we all carry guns? The question's so loaded,
It's a wonder the blogosphere never exploded.

Is the Second Amendment a good lodestar
For judging how sane today's gun laws are?
When the Founding Fathers charted our nation,
They sought to shield states from domination.
The settlers feared that a monarch named George
Was bound and determined to try and disgorge
Them of weapons they needed to mount a defense.
So they wanted a safeguard. That made common sense.
For militias, guns were a clear necessity,
Since militias provided the states with security.

In the nineteen thirties, Miller got indicted.
His sawed-off shotgun was the thing that invited
A dispute because of this troublesome fact:
Having it was against the Firearms Act.
The trial judge ruled that the law's prohibition
Violated the U.S. Constitution,
Since the Second Amendment made it clear
That gun owners had nothing to fear.
On direct appeal, the High Court decided:
"One's passion for guns must remain unrequited --
If they're not for suppressing an insurrection,

Or designed for repelling a foreign invasion,
This Court will not grant them any protection.
They do not belong in a person's possession.
The Second Amendment does not guarantee
The right to keep guns that aren't military.
A musket and a bayonet
Are more in line with our mind-set."[1]

That topic was settled, till two thousand eight, when
The Court took a look at the question again.
The NRA had entered the fray --
They wanted gun laws to go away.
They found a D.C. man who sought the right
To keep a handgun in his home at night.
But the District had a strict regulation
Prohibiting in-home handgun possession.
They argued one's right to self-defense
Is part of Amendment Two, and hence,
They asked the Top Court in the nation
If it would zap the regulation.
Dick Heller was the plaintiff's name.
The case would gain him immortal fame.

How would it go, the press wanted to know --
Would right- and left-wingers go toe to toe?
Would it turn on constitutionality,
Or fall prey to political policy?
Its ruling displayed the Court's deep divide,
With only five Jurists on the NRA's side.
Justice Scalia got to carry the ball.
His opinion ran sixty-four pages in all.
Said Scalia, "Here's our in-depth examination
Of the Framers' rusty gun rights declaration.
We did not want to jump the gun, so we waited
For a chance to show it's not antiquated.
We need to decide if a party of one
Has a guaranteed right to keep a handgun.
After searching through history thoroughly,
We find self-defense rights are mandatory.

The Amendment provides a guarantee,
Which applies to you and applies to me,
That all of us may possess and carry
Unless there's a reason to the contrary,
Like mental illness or a record tellin'
That a person has been adjudged a felon.
Second Amendment rights aren't unlimited --
So many things can still be prohibited.
We would not forbid certain regulations,
Like no-go places and concealed-carry limitations.
And weapons that aren't in common use
Can be banned as likely to lead to abuse."

Scalia relied on public opinion,
Not the Amendment, vis-à-vis the handgun:
"Americans deem handguns the quintessential
Weapons. For self-defense, they're seen as essential.
The ban on handguns in one's residence
Won't pass muster, we say with confidence.
Though we understand there's a deadly scourge
Of gun violence lots of folks want to purge,
The way to address it is not prohibition,
But licensing and handgun registration.
Is the Second Amendment *passé* and outmoded
In a country whose cops carry guns that are loaded,
With a standing army that's the pride of our nation --
Shouldn't all this suffice to afford us protection?
That's debatable, but to be quite succinct,
It's not this Court's job to pronounce it extinct."

Four Justices dissented --
They were quite discontented.
They said, "The Amendment had only one role --
To keep central government under control,
So settlers wouldn't be left defenseless.
Banning all weapons would have been senseless.
But colonial laws did contain gritty
Laws against bearing guns within the city.
Thus, it's not the case that history

Is the start and the end of our inquiry.
Five Justices ought not to pull the trigger,
Lest this country's problems only grow bigger."[2]

Guns for Everyone

Heller left a burning question on the table:
Did it mean that state courts would be unable
To retain a law banning anyone
Who lives in a city from having a gun?
Heller dealt with a federal entity --
A special district we call D.C.,
And for most of American history,
The Bill of Rights governed just U.S. territory.

The Civil War ended with an innovation --
The Fourteenth Amendment's declaration
That the states shall not deprive any person
Of certain key rights that freedom depends on.
But it took many decades for the Bill of Rights
To seep into state courts. There were lots of fights.
The High Court extended it, gradually,
Granting each separate right selectively,
Until most of Amendments One through Ten
In state courthouses had been born again.

Right-wing Justices had resisted the trend,
And seemed unwilling, on this question, to bend.
So some thought their reading of Amendment Two
Would restrict gun rights to the chosen few
Who lived their lives on federal land,
Such as D.C., where guns had been banned.

Then Otis McDonald's case came along,
And the elderly gentleman joined the throng
Of voices who wished city gun bans to end,
Since he feared that his home he might need to defend.
Otis lived in Chicago, in a rough part of town,
Where lots of violent crimes had gone down.
But the city's law banned all gun possession,
So voiding the law became his obsession.

At the High Court, the right-wingers held sway --

Their five-four majority gave them their way.
"Justice Black," they noted, "had long advocated
The first ten amendments be incorporated
In the Fourteenth Amendment and applied to the states.
But this limited test had been put in its place:
'Is the right fundamental to liberty,
Or rooted in this nation's history'?"

The Court debated, should each city and state
Be free to fine-tune and differentiate
Its laws based on state and local conditions
And persist in taking separate positions?
Or is the right to bear arms so fundamental
That eroding the right is too consequential?

Alito wrote on behalf of the five
Jurists who sought to keep gun rights alive.
"It is clear," he stated with certainty,
"Gun rights are so basic to liberty,
They must be observed in a state and city
Just as in a federal entity.
But this is not a doomsday proclamation
That imperils all local regulation.
We'll leave it to each state and city
To work out all the nitty-gritty."

Justice Stevens filed a blistering dissent
Castigating the plurality's argument:
"What's meant by the term 'liberty'?", said he.
"It's a term of dynamic vitality.
We must not confine it to history,
Which included the scourge of slavery.
An all-purpose, top-down view of liberty
May end in failure and futility.
True, guns might be used for self-defense,
But there's often another consequence --
Violence, destruction, and devastation
Are part of the 'liberty' equation."[3]

Guns and Domestic Violence

Now that the Court had finally spoken,
Did it mean *all* old gun laws were broken?
A national law got re-tested when
Feds went after James Alvin Castleman.

His saga began in two thousand and one,
When he wound up in court for what he had done.
Charged with committing "domestic assault,"
He told the judge the whole thing was his fault.
Castleman never offered a denial --
That way, he avoided a messy trial.
All that's clear from the record is that his wife
Came through the ordeal without losing her life.
One can only imagine his elation
When his sentence was just a year's probation.

The Tennessee law said if you're convicted
Of said crime, gun ownership is interdicted.
He could no longer buy guns under his name,
Yet his wife bought them for him all the same.
Then she turned the guns over to her spouse,
Who stored the contraband inside their house.

He ran a black market gun enterprise,
And sold a gun used in a homicide.
The couple still lived in that southern state
When the Feds tracked him down in two thousand eight.

A grand jury indicted the married man
For running afoul of a federal ban
On possessing guns with the prior offense
Of a crime of "domestic violence,"
Where any of the guns traverse
State lines in interstate commerce.

But James Alvin Castleman had the gall
To argue, "I shouldn't be punished at all,

Since you can't prove that my prior offense
Involved any sort of violence.
Violence is defined in the federal law
As 'physical force' -- put that in your craw!
What if I simply poisoned her drink?
That shouldn't land me in the clink!
Plus, the Gun Control Act denies my right
To keep and bear arms in case of a fight."

The High Court looked with great skepticism
On Castleman's proposed catechism.
"Notwithstanding his logic and antics,
He won't get off simply due to semantics.
He was convicted of knowingly
Causing her bodily injury.
That means he had to use physical force,
Which amounts to domestic violence, of course.
This Court adopts an expansive view
Of what an abuser would have to do.
The words 'physical force' need not be included
In the law of the state where abuse is precluded
For the case to fall under the Gun Control Act
That the Congress so wisely chose to enact.
His prior conviction suffices for when
He is sentenced to go to the federal pen.

"As for the law's constitutionality,
His cursory challenge lacks credibility.
Guns when combined with domestic strife
Are a recipe leading to loss of life.
Officers' lives are placed in grave danger
When called to the home of an armed stranger.
The Second Amendment does not forbid
Banning guns to protect a spouse or kid."[4]

Don't Lie for the Other Guy

While the Feds were checking out Bruce to see
If he'd committed a bank robbery,
They came across papers that proved this fact:
He'd broken the federal Gun Control Act.
When he bought a Glock, he filled out a paper
At a federally licensed gun shop dealer,
Saying, "I am the person buying the gun,"
When the truth was, he bought it *for* someone.
He tried to wriggle off the hook
By saying, "That person is not a crook,
A drug addict or mentally ill.
I simply saved him a trip, if you will."

Said the Court, "We won't allow that excuse.
If we did, the Act would be of no use,
Since the info is needed by Feds to track
Guns used in crimes when they're checking back.
Otherwise, only numbskulls would fail
To avoid leaving a paper trail.
Straw purchasers will be sent to the clink.
Bruce has broken the law -- that's what we think."

Bruce wished to game the system if he could.
This ex-cop was too slick for his own good.
Instead, he wound up strengthening the law:
Gun buyers get in trouble if they're straw.[5]

Chapter VI. Crime And Punishment

Sixth Amendment: In all criminal prosecutions, the accused shall enjoy the right to a speedy and public trial, by an impartial jury ....

Eighth Amendment: Excessive bail shall not be required, nor excessive fines imposed, nor cruel and unusual punishment inflicted.

Fourteenth Amendment: ... No State shall make or enforce any law which shall abridge the privileges or immunities of citizens of the United States, nor shall any State deprive any person of life, liberty, or property, without due process of law; nor deny to any person within its jurisdiction the equal protection of the laws.

Juries and Liberty

Gary Duncan was only nineteen
When he drove down a winding highway unseen
By those standing at the side of the road,
And saw an encounter about to explode --
His two younger cousins in conversation
With four youths as pale as the Aryan Nation.
His kin had opted to integrate
An all-white school in that southern state.
Duncan knew there'd been incidents at school,
And racial tensions provided the fuel.

He stopped to pull his cousins out of danger,
Lest they fall victim to an angry stranger.
While corralling his kin, he brushed his arm
Against a white boy, though he meant no harm.
But the white boys claimed he'd slapped the elbow
Of one highly agitated white fellow.

Duncan was charged with simple battery,
A misdemeanor bearing a penalty
Of up to two years' imprisonment
In case of an adverse judgment.
He asked the judge for a jury trial,
But that request met with denial,
Since the Louisiana Constitution
Limited the right to that institution.

Though the sentence for battery could be two years in jail,
Unless charged with a felony, his request had to fail.
The trial judge convicted him on the spot.
The sentence he gave was not a lot --
Just sixty days in the House of Correction.
Duncan wouldn't accept it without objection.
His persistent lawyer would not stop short --
He brought the case to the country's Top Court.

The High Court took up the following query:
Does the Sixth Amendment right to a jury
Apply in state courts to a serious crime
Where a person's exposed to some heavy jail time,
And is this right so fundamental
That it trumps state law, like the right to counsel?

Said the Court, "The founding fathers felt very wary
Of giving too much power to the judiciary.
They wanted involvement by the community
To offer defendants some immunity
From oppression by a hostile government
And judges who might not be independent.
They deemed that the right to trial by jury
Is essential for our liberty.
Thus, we conclude that state sentencing laws
Must obey the Fourteenth Amendment's Due Process
Clause.
And we now hold that in all U.S. states
A jury trial for serious crimes rates
As a fundamental right to aid the defense
In crimes that carry a lengthy sentence."[1]

Death Is Different

The Eighth Amendment has a very long history,
Yet its meaning remains an inscrutable mystery.
We know little about the Framers' intent
In choosing the words in the Eighth Amendment.
What was "cruel and unusual" meant to convey?
Might they have expressed it in a more precise way?
Were they simply seeking a lasting solution
That banned barbarous modes of execution,
Or were they concerned, at that point in time,
With making the punishment fit the crime?

Should the word "cruel" over time remain static
Like an old hat in somebody's attic,
Or evolve as standards of decency
Progress in a maturing society?

From all the debate about capital punishment,
There's one thing we know -- death is different.
What makes it different is not just morality --
The thing that stands out is its very finality.
Due to human error and false testimony,
Mistaken convictions are a real possibility.
Many inmates have been freed from death row
After courts found them innocent and let them go.
Some have gone free after their DNA
Proved they should never have been sent away.

In nineteen hundred and seventy-two,
The Court created a Waterloo
When it struck down state laws across the land,
And stated that all executions were banned,
Since state laws gave juries too much discretion
When voting to hand out the ultimate sanction.
The Court said, "The current process is frightening,
Since it's random like being struck by lightning."[2]

In seventy-six, a Georgia case reached the Court

Asking the Jurists to hand down their retort
To these questions: "Is a death sentence *per se*
Banned by the Amendment -- is it yea or nay?
And if not, might a law with a tight procedure
In lieu of a standardless law be the cure
For the problems the Court found four years ago
When it stopped executions for all on death row?
Has the public's perspective on decency
Evolved to the point where it's heresy
To ever impose the death penalty
Because it's a blot on humanity?"

Said the Court, "We can't get ahead of society
By adopting a stance of unjustified piety,
Since many among us would find such an action
Removes an appropriate criminal sanction.
When a law-making body enacts a penalty,
The first thing we do is presume its validity.
We find Georgia's new law meets the requirements
Of the Eighth and also the Fourteenth Amendments.
It's good that the process is bifurcated,
So guilt and sentencing are separated.
Once the person's found guilty, there's a second stage
Where both sides a battle royal can wage
As they bring up more facts from defendant's past
To weigh whether his life should continue to last.
But no sentence of death may ever be given
Unless one of a set list of facts has been proven.
This final procedure provides the key
To ensuring a standard of decency.
We approve of this law without objection,
Since it carefully limits a jury's discretion.
It reduces the chance of a sentence that fairly
Can be seen as capricious or arbitrary."[3]

A Crime by Any Other Name

No doubt, Apprendi did a despicable action,
Made a hateful statement, and then gave a retraction.
But there remained questions about his intent.
Was he merely drunk, or was a hate crime meant?
He fired at the home of some folks who were black.
At the sentencing hearing, he took his words back.
His witnesses said he held no racial bias,
Though he couldn't stay sober. No one called him pious.

When the grand jury handed down their indictment,
The crimes they charged weren't about racial incitement.
They accused him of shooting and weapons possession,
And to those charges he made a full confession.
He pled to possessing a weapon, which then
Carried a sentence of just five-to-ten.

But he and the D.A. no way could agree
On a sentence enhancement of ten-to-twenty
For use of a gun in a nasty hate crime.
He said, "I shouldn't have to do that kind of time.
Since it wasn't what the grand jury found,
I should not by the hate crime law be bound."
For Apprendi, the hate crime law spelled trouble.
If found guilty of that, his sentence could double.

The trial judge held a sentencing hearing
To see if the facts supported a finding
That Apprendi was imbued with hate,
And fired the shots to intimidate.
Said the judge, "I think that's true, more likely than not,
So I'm adding two years, which is not such a lot.
I'll order jail time of twelve years in all,
'Cause for the hate crime he's taking a fall."

Was "more likely than not" a serious flaw
In New Jersey's creative hate crime law?
Their law permitted a judge to affirm

That defendants should get an extended term
If he finds racial bias by a "preponderance"
After sifting through all the evidence.
Did it violate one's jury right
To allow a burden of proof so slight?
Was New Jersey's law a kind of shell game
That labeled a crime with a different name
By calling it a "sentencing factor"
So the judge gets to say who'll be deemed a bad actor?

Said the High Court, "While a rose by any name smells sweet,
In America, a D.A. must his burden meet.
If he can't prove a crime beyond a reasonable doubt,
In our system of justice, we must toss the case out.
A trademark of the American way
Is to let the jury have their say
With a standard of proof that's high enough
To make upping a sentence really tough.
That's what the Sixth Amendment requires,
Though it may not be what the D.A. desires.

"Any fact that increases the penalty range
Is part of the crime, since the sentence can change.
In most states, an important element
Of a hate crime is the suspect's intent.
When a judge makes that sort of factual finding,
We don't believe it should be binding.
That's a violation of our basic laws,
And the Fourteenth Amendment's Due Process Clause."[4]

Juries and Mandatory Minimums

In the old days, here's how it used to be:
Each crime came with a discrete penalty.
Today's sentencing laws may offer a range,
So based on the facts, the sentence can change.
Plus, many laws will add on a kicker
Where an inmate's release would come slower, not quicker.
Say the person committing the crime used a gun --
Then more time could be added onto the first one.

Some crimes come pre-loaded with a "mandatory minimum,"
Though they may not carry a lid for the maximum.
Are such sentencing schemes required to fight
Inner-city gun crimes and to curb city blight?
When debating these schemes, scholars disagree,
Siding pro and con on their efficacy.
One said they're as useful as a moose's hat-rack.
Debates on this topic are bound to be back.

Now Alleyne and his bud hatched a nasty plan
To waylay a store manager and then rob the man
As he drove to the bank to deposit some money.
Their plan was so cynical, it wasn't funny.
They pretended to have trouble with their car,
And asked for his help before he'd gone far.
When he stopped to give aid, they approached with a gun.
He gave them the cash, and it looked like they'd won.

Then a witness tied Alleyne to the crime,
And his fortunes turned around on a dime.
He got hauled in for the federal offense
Of gun use in a crime of violence.
The law had a mandatory minimum
Of five years, with no cap for a maximum.
Plus, the minimum would increase to seven

Anytime the culprit brandished a weapon.

The jury said that he'd used a gun,
But didn't find that he "brandished" one.
Yet, the judge ruled, "Sentencing is up to me,
And there was 'brandishing' from what I can see.
So I'm setting his sentence at seven years
Despite the view of that jury of his peers."
But Alleyne objected, with a sense of resentment,
"Judicial fact-finding violates my Sixth Amendment
Right to have an impartial jury
Decide facts that affect my penalty."

The Supremes stepped into the testy turf war
Over whether the judge sets the sentence or
It's the jury's province to decide
Any facts to be used as a sentencing guide.

Said the Court, "This matter hinges on
Whether the brandishing of the gun
Was an ingredient of the crime
Or a sentencing factor in upping the time.
The historic role of the jury
Is to guard against tyranny.
They are the bulwark of our liberty --
The Framers brought it from the old country.
.
"We find that brandishing is a part of this crime,
And the jury must find it to up the base time.
In such a case, the accused need not worry --
That decision must be left to the jury.
The fact must be proved beyond a reasonable doubt,
Since that's what the burden of proof is about.
While it's true a judge has sentencing discretion,
This judge fell afoul of the Constitution
When said he based his sentencing decision
On a fact that's within the jury's discretion."

The dissent pointed out, since the law had no cap

On the maximum time, had the judge shut his trap
And not explained that he'd made a finding,
The seven-year sentence would have been binding.[5]

Punishing the Dealers

Here are two problems plaguing society:
Drug addiction and lack of sobriety.
Congress set out to go after the dealers
By cracking down hard on those free-wheelers.
In eighty-six, Congress upped the ante
By enacting a so-called enhanced penalty
For convictions where the drug abuser
Died from the drug sold to that user.

Mister Banka had a nasty drug habit.
He went on a binge, since he couldn't help it.
There were so many drugs found in his tissue
That the experts could not resolve the issue
Of which of those substances did him in,
Though the last drug he took was heroin.
Banka's wife knew who sold him the final batch,
So the dealer proved easy for Feds to catch.

Where death results, the revised law requires
At least twenty years to be served behind bars.
This raises a question about causation --
What percentage of the fatal equation
Must be traced to the addict's ingestion
Of the particular drug in question?
Would fifty percent prove to be sufficient?
Would just five percent be too deficient?

The judge told the jury, "Here's what you must agree
If you vote to impose the enhanced penalty:
That the drug the defendant sold the deceased
Helped to cause his death at the very least."
In truth, the jurors had no way to surmise
Which of the substances led to his demise.
They ultimately announced in one breath,
"The heroin certainly caused his death."

The nine Justices undertook to decide

If the jury instruction was just too cockeyed.
Said the Court, "Banka engaged in lots of drug binges,
But it's unclear to us on which drug his death hinges.
The toxicologist was mystified,
And could not pinpoint why Banka died,
Except to say that a drug interaction
Might have triggered a severe reaction.
There's no evidence that he would have survived,
Assuming the heroin never arrived.
So where using the drug the dealer sold
Did not suffice to knock him out cold,
And could not be deemed an independent cause,
The enhanced penalty is at odds with the laws."[6]

Insanity and the Death Penalty

The mentally ill reside under a cloud --
Scant few are willing to discuss it out loud.
Their symptoms might not stand out in a crowd,
So shadows and secrecy often shroud
Those enduring a severe illness of the brain,
Often left without help in unbearable pain.

Yet, victims who take proper medication
Are likely to find it to be their salvation.
Modern drugs work well to suppress a delusion
That causes great angst and disabling confusion.
Left untreated, victims may succumb to the voices
That all but eliminate sensible choices.

The illnesses causing the worst sorts of mania
Are bipolar disease and schizophrenia.
These rarely become pronounced and full-blown
Till a youth matures and is fully grown.
They can also develop much later in life,
In response to a trauma or some extreme strife.

Take the case of a prisoner named Alvin Ford
Who believed he held powers like those of the Lord.
He committed a murder while seemingly sane,
But in prison, his mental state started to wane.
He blamed the prison guards for collusion
In a murderous plot that was just a delusion.
A shrink concluded that his form of mania
Resembled severe paranoid schizophrenia.
His disordered thinking made him so weak
That eventually, he could barely speak.

Florida's Governor said he had to die,
But his lawyer gave it one last college try
By asking the High Court to answer this question:
Does the Eighth Amendment forbid execution
On the grounds that it's cruel and inhumane

To kill a person thought to be insane?

Said the Court, "The Governor's order has a flaw --
The English banned the practice under common law.
Today, it's banned in all fifty states,
So his decision deviates.
Since it serves no goal of retribution,
To crime, it offers no solution.
Due to progress in our maturing society,
Fairness in the law has evolved substantially
Since we last viewed inflicting the death penalty
On a prisoner who had lost his sanity.
We have finally recognized, in short,
The Eighth Amendment applies in state court.
It changes the game so significantly,
That we now proclaim unequivocally:
The Eighth Amendment places a ban
On executing an insane man."[7]

Retardation and Execution

Jones and Atkins pulled off a robbery,
Then added homicide to their crime spree.
Each said that the other had done the shooting,
Though both admitted to doing the looting.
Jones gave the jury a better spiel,
And the jury figured he was for real.
Atkins could do little more than sputter,
So the jury found that he did the murder,
And due to his alleged brutality
Imposed the ultimate penalty.

Atkins' lawyer began to exhort
The judges on the appellate court.
"You can't execute him," the lawyer said,
"My client is mentally retarded."
To that plea, the state court turned a deaf ear.
But this was a case the Supremes would hear.

In *Atkins*, the High Court set out to opine
On a perp whose I.Q. was just fifty-nine.
The Court asked, "Would imposing the death penalty
Be too lacking in reliability,
Since there is a distinct possibility
That folks having impaired ability
Are inclined to confess unwittingly
To crimes where they lack culpability?
And should their diminished self-control
Mean their fault is less than the average criminal?"

Said the Court, "Our system becomes too aggressive
When we impose sanctions clearly excessive.
There are times when we've granted leniency
Due to evolving standards of decency.
That's what we did in the case of insanity --
The outcome was prompted by simple humanity.

"Two main rationales underpin execution --

The goals of deterrence and retribution.
But these rationales fail miserably
When deciding death eligibility
For convicts who are mentally retarded.
The old rule allowing it must be discarded.
More and more states, from the trends we can see
Don't execute those with I.Q.s under seventy.
This means the practice is truly unusual.
We therefore declare it unconstitutional.

The problem with enforcing this interdiction
Is the lack of a widely shared definition
Stating which offenders are so impaired
That they qualify to have their lives spared.
Each state must devise its own prescription
To use in applying this restriction."[8]

Too Young to Die?

When Chris Simmons was only seventeen,
He acted out something despicably mean.
He killed a woman with no provocation,
And afterwards, felt a sense of elation.
No one knows if he was just badly misled,
Or had something terribly wrong with his head.
Was it youth or malevolence that caused him to act?
A jury found the latter, as a matter of fact.
The jurors agreed, the best solution
For Chris Simmons would be execution.

But the *Atkins* ruling on retardation
Reflected a change in the calculation.
The Court deferred to the trend and direction
Of states banning juvenile execution.
"A national consensus has accrued:
Execution of juveniles must be eschewed.
The Eighth Amendment has interdicted
'Unusual' punishments from being inflicted.
Since just three states still kill a juvenile,
It's clear, the practice has gone out of style.
The trend toward abolition
Has a simple explanation.
Their innate absence of maturity
Oft comes with irresponsibility.
Thus, when their conduct is indefensible,
Compared to adults, it's less reprehensible.
Our evolving standards of decency
Call for an end to the death penalty
When the offender is under eighteen,
Since no gain for society can be seen.
Juveniles, though they may appear depraved,
In time might become much better behaved."[9]

A Fatal Number

Freddie Hall and his bud did some really bad stuff.
So a jury said, "We've heard more than enough."
They sentenced both men to the death penalty.
Freddie's lawyer petitioned for leniency.

At resentencing, his lawyer got a chance
To bring in mitigating evidence
Of his childhood and mental condition,
Hoping to alter the jury's position.
Each night, his Mom tied him to the bed
To restrain the boy who was soft in the head.
She beat him once or twice every day.
Hall's childhood was filled with pain and dismay.
His teachers said he was always slow --
There were too many things he didn't know.
He could not learn to read or write;
No one ever considered him bright.
He had trouble forming words in his head --
It was hard to make out the things he said.
A bevy of specialists testified
Hall's retardation could not be denied.
He could not aid his lawyer with his trial;
Conversing with him proved very futile.
Still, the second jury went right ahead
And recommended that he should be dead.

On appeal to Florida's highest court,
Five of seven judges had this retort:
"We give this new evidence little weight,
So we're still inclined to agree with the State."

But Freddie's case came up for review
After the Supremes, in 2002,
Said convicted felons can't be discarded
If they're diagnosed as being retarded.

The state court agreed to decide whether Hall

Qualified to be deemed retarded at all.
State law relied heavily on one's I.Q.,
Assuming that this single factor would do.
Hall's I.Q. tested at seventy-one,
So the Florida court ruled, "Now we're done.
Hall is excluded on account of his score,
Since we'll accept seventy, and not a point more.
Once that threshold has been met,
There's nothing else we need to vet."

When the Court ruled in *Atkins*, it had demurred,
Allowing the judgment to be deferred
As to whether one number could neatly define
Retardation and draw a dividing line.
But when Florida set a strict cutoff test,
The Supremes decided, "By now, it's best
To eliminate the unfettered discretion
Of each state to devise its own definition.
We cannot simply sit back and slumber
While a state court puts all its faith in a number.
While choosing a number would really be nice,
I.Q. testing is far too imprecise.
Mental retardation
Needs more explanation:
It's not a number, but a condition
To be determined by a clinician.

"It degrades a trial's integrity
If we impose the death penalty
On folks with mental disability,
Who could not impact a trial's accuracy.
The Eighth Amendment's protection of dignity
Reflects the Nation we are and aspire to be.
Evolving standards of decency
Mark the progress of our society.
The Sunshine State's rigid numerical rule
Is both unusual and cruel.
That offends the Constitution,
So it's not an acceptable solution."[10]

Some Parting Words

So what did the High Court have to say
To help guide one's actions day by day?
After seeing what factors are at play,
Here are some nuggets you might take away.

A cop must not stop cars for no good reason,
Since on drivers, there's no open season,
Save at a checkpoint to assess sobriety.
But that must be brief and not cause anxiety.
If they suspect a traffic infraction,
Cops are allowed to take limited action --
They can ask for your license and registration
Without incurring the Court's indignation.
They can also make you step out of your car
For officer safety. That's not going too far.
But they can't search your car without your consent --
That's beyond the scope of the Fourth Amendment.

A stop-and-frisk, if there's grounds for suspicion,
Is allowed to be part of an officer's mission.
But it is required to be short in duration
To avoid causing citizens consternation.
And cops must limit their intrusions
To outerwear pat-downs to check for weapons.
Now once the brief stop appears to be over,
Folks should be free to leave and end the encounter.

Police must not employ deadly force
Against fleeing suspects unless, of course,
They pose a very significant threat
To safety that can't be otherwise met.
Regardless, it's never a wise thing to flee
If you want to ensure your security.

If a suspect is lawfully under arrest
For a serious crime, the Court says it's best
To permit cops to swab for DNA

YOUR RIGHTS WHEN STOPPED BY POLICE
Nancy E. Albert

Without obtaining the suspect's OK.
If a driver reeks of alcohol
When a cop pays him or her a call,
A warrant's required if cops want to go in
With a needle and puncture a person's skin.
Refuseniks can get their license revoked,
But without a warrant, they can't be poked.
However, requiring a driver to blow
In a straw is allowed, and not a no-go.

A search may be done incident to an arrest,
But only for items kept close to one's vest.
If an item's beyond the suspect's reach,
The warrantless search would be a breach.
And cops can't search your cellphone in an arrest
Without violating a due process test.

If the cops tell you that you're under arrest,
Remaining silent would be best,
Since anything that you're tempted to say
Could be used against you at a later day.
But go ahead and assert your right
To confer with a lawyer, be it day or night.
Don't ever cop to a guilty plea
Before getting advice from an attorney.
You've got the right to request a jury
If exposed to a serious penalty.
And if you think the cops have gone too far,
Remember, the Court says there is no bar
To filing a lawsuit to make them pay
For behaving in a lawless way.

Since your home is where you have a right to be,
Warrantless snooping invades your privacy.
Agents can't employ helpers having four paws
Without brazenly breaking no-trespassing laws,
And high-tech gizmos are not allowed
To peer into places hidden from a crowd.

At work, if you're using your boss's devices,
A word to the wise, we hope, suffices --
Be aware that your boss may have authority
To audit and monitor your activity.

All adults have the right to possess and carry,
Unless there's a reason to the contrary,
Like mental illness or a record tellin'
That a person's been adjudged a felon.
But the Court approves of some regulations,
Like no-go places and licensing limitations.
Plus, the Second Amendment does not forbid
Banning guns near a battered spouse or a kid.

Amendment One means you can speak your piece,
Even when you're talking to the police.
That rule may be all well and good,
But speaking out could be misunderstood.
Therefore, you're well-advised to wait
At least until your first court date,
Since anytime you diss a cop,
He's apt to try and make you stop.

We hope this helps to shine some light
And aid in safeguarding the basic right
To justice for each citizen.
If we've furthered that goal, we say, "Amen."

Notes and Holdings

The citations to opinions follow the format used by the courts. For example, *Mapp v. Ohio*, 367 U.S. 643 (1961), means that the United States Supreme Court decided the case in 1961, and it was printed in volume 367 of the United States Reports, beginning at page 643. The same principle applies to the Supreme Court Reporter, referred to in citations as "S.Ct.".

I. Freedom of Speech and Breaching the Peace

1. *Cantwell v. Connecticut*, 310 U.S. 296 (1940). Cantwell was charged with the common law offense of inciting a breach of the peace. In a unanimous opinion, the United States Supreme Court held that a person could not be convicted of inciting a breach of the peace for exercising his rights to freedom of speech and freedom of religion, provided there is no clear and present danger to public peace and order.

However, the Court left the door open for states to enact statutes narrowly drawn to define and punish specific conduct that constitutes a clear and present danger.

2. *Chaplinsky v. State of New Hampshire*, 315 U.S. 568 (1942). A unanimous Court held that New Hampshire's name-calling statute did not violate the Constitution because so-called "fighting words" by their very nature lead to disorderly conduct by those against whom the epithets are directed.

3. *Lewis v. New Orleans*, 415 U.S. 130 (1974). The High Court held that the New Orleans ordinance interfered with protected speech, and therefore, was overbroad in violation of the First and Fourteenth Amendments in that it had a wider sweep than the constitutional definition of "fighting words" announced in *Chaplinsky*.

4. The High Court, in *Houston, Texas v. Hill*, 482 U.S. 451 (1987), decided that a municipal ordinance making it unlawful "to interrupt any policeman in the execution of his duty" is substantially overbroad, and therefore invalid under the First and Fourteenth Amendments to the United States Constitution. "[T]he First Amendment protects a significant amount of verbal criticism and challenge directed at police officers", the Court said. The Court added, "Today's decision reflects the constitutional requirement that, in the face of verbal challenges to police action, officers and municipalities must respond with restraint."

However, several Justices writing separately in *Houston v. Hill* argued that, while they agreed on striking down the Houston ordinance, they did not believe that *Lewis v. City of New Orleans* (see note 3 above) had been correctly decided. They said Mrs. Lewis had engaged in "fighting words" intended to interfere with the performance by the police officer of his lawful duties.

5. *Edwards v. South Carolina*, 372 U.S. 229 (1963). In an 8-1 opinion, the United States Supreme Court held that a group of 187 civil rights protestors had the right, under the First and Fourteenth Amendments to the U.S. Constitution, to march around the State Capitol carrying placards, to sing, to clap their hands, and to stamp their feet after being allowed onto Capitol grounds by police. "[I]n arresting, convicting, and punishing the petitioners under the circumstances disclosed by the record, South Carolina infringed the petitioners' constitutionally protected rights of free speech, free assembly, and freedom to petition for redress of their grievances", the Court said.

As the Court noted, the South Carolina Supreme Court had acknowledged that the offense of breaching the peace, which the state adopted as part of the common law inherited from England, was so generalized as to be "not susceptible of exact definition."

The Court added that violating a police order to disperse within fifteen minutes, in the absence of evidence that the group was disrupting pedestrian or vehicular traffic, is not grounds for arrest.

The Court handed down a pair of decisions in a similar case two years after deciding *Edwards*. In *Cox v. Louisiana (Cox I)*, 379 U.S. 536 (1965), 23 college students, directed by a chapter of the Congress of Racial Equality (CORE), were arrested for violating a Louisiana "disturbing the peace" statute during a march to protest racial segregation. A unanimous Court held that the statute violates the First and Fourteenth Amendments to the U.S. Constitution because it sweeps so broadly that it prohibits freedom of speech and assembly. The *Cox* court concluded that, while laws may limit the time, place, duration or manner of using the streets for public assemblies, it is unconstitutional to accord unbridled discretion to local officials.

In a companion case, *Cox v. Louisiana (Cox II)*, 379 U.S. 559 (1965), the High Court discussed the effect of the sheriff's order to disperse after the police chief had previously agreed to allow the group to demonstrate. The Court held that police must give fair notice that permission to demonstrate is revoked before they can begin arresting demonstrators for picketing.

II. Perspectives on Privacy

1. In *Payton v. New York*, 445 U.S. 573 (1980), the U.S. Supreme Court overturned a New York statute authorizing police officers to enter a private residence to make a routine felony arrest. The Court held that the Fourth Amendment, made applicable to the states by the Fourteenth Amendment, prohibits the police from making a warrantless and nonconsensual entry into a suspect's home in order to make a routine felony arrest.

However, the Court has carved out an exception for "exigent circumstances," such as when someone is in imminent danger, or when police are in "hot pursuit" of a fleeing felon. For a discussion of what qualifies as "exigent circumstances, " see *Welsh v. Wisconsin*, 466 U.S. 740 (1984).

2. *Minnesota v. Olson*, 495 U.S. 91 (1990), held that an overnight guest in a residence has the sort of expectation of privacy that the Fourth Amendment protects.

3. *Mapp v. Ohio*, 367 U.S. 643 (1961). The issue in *Mapp* was whether the Exclusionary Rule, which forbad the use of unlawfully obtained evidence in federal criminal cases, should apply in state court prosecutions. In a 6-3 decision, the U.S. Supreme Court held that all evidence obtained by searches and seizures conducted in violation of the Constitution is inadmissible in state courts, since the Fourth Amendment right to privacy is enforceable against the states through the Due Process Clause of the Fourteenth Amendment. In addition, the Court held that the Exclusionary Rule "is an essential part of both the Fourth and Fourteenth Amendments".

The *Mapp* decision overruled *Wolf v. Colorado*, 338 U.S. 25 (1949), which had held that in prosecutions conducted in state courts for state crimes, the Fourteenth Amendment to the U.S. Constitution does not forbid the admission of evidence obtained by an unreasonable search or seizure.

4. *Katz v. United States*, 389 U.S. 347 (1967). In a 7-1 decision (Justice Thurgood Marshall took no part in deciding this case), the Court held: the Fourth Amendment's ban on unreasonable searches and seizures requires that law enforcement officers obtain a search warrant before using electronic surveillance to listen in on a person's telephone conversations.

The Court deemed the fact that the surveillance did not involve a physical penetration of the space to be irrelevant, because "the Fourth Amendment protects people, not places." This statement effectively overruled a prior case, *Olmstead v. United States*, 277 U.S. 438

(1928), which held that the absence of physical penetration of property foreclosed Fourth Amendment inquiry.

The Government had argued, in *Katz*, that a telephone booth, unlike a home, did not merit constitutional protection. The Court disagreed, finding that a person has a constitutionally protected reasonable expectation of privacy in a phone booth.

5. *Terry v. Ohio*, 392 U.S. 1 (1968). A 9-1 majority of the Justices held that the Fourth Amendment permits a brief seizure of a person for the purpose of conducting a pat-down for weapons, as long as the officer has a "reasonable suspicion" that the suspect is committing or is about to commit a crime. However, the pat-down must be limited to feeling the suspect's outer clothing. *Terry* allows a temporary detention without a warrant on the basis of "reasonable suspicion" -- a lower standard than "probable cause." This narrow exception to the Fourth Amendment was announced for the first time in *Terry*.

Justice John Marshall Harlan (II), in a concurring opinion, predicted that "what is said by this Court today will serve as initial guidelines for law enforcement ... as this important new field of law develops."

Justice William O. Douglas filed the lone dissent in *Terry*.

Note that the term "probable cause," which is found in the Fourth Amendment, requires more than mere suspicion. Probable cause exists where the facts and circumstances within the officers' knowledge and of which they have reasonably trustworthy information are sufficient in themselves to warrant a person of reasonable caution in the belief that an offense has been or is being committed. See *Brinegar v. United States*, 338 U.S. 160 (1949).

6. *Navarette v. California*, 134 S.Ct. 1126 (2014). In a 5-4 decision, the High Court held that, so long as a 9-1-1

caller claiming to be an eyewitness provides the car's make, plate number and location, the anonymous allegation of a single instance of reckless driving supports a traffic stop by police. The Court justified the investigative stop on the ground that, under the totality of circumstances in this case, the officer had reasonable suspicion that the driver was intoxicated.

Justice Antonin Scalia, writing on behalf of the four dissenters, argued that the officers' five-minute surveillance of the vehicle demonstrated that the anonymous 9-1-1 tip was inaccurate and therefore, unreliable. He contended that the majority's opinion departed from the Court's normal Fourth Amendment requirement that anonymous tips must be corroborated in order to justify an investigative stop.

7. *Delaware v. Prouse*, 440 U.S. 648 (1979). The Court held that, unless there is at least articulable and reasonable suspicion of a licensing violation or other crime, stopping a car and detaining the driver in order to check his license and registration are unreasonable under the Fourth Amendment.

Nonetheless, in *Heien v. North Carolina*, 135 S.Ct. 530 (2014), the Court held that an officer did not violate the Fourth Amendment when he stopped a motorist for having a broken brake light in North Carolina even though that state's law allowed motorists to drive with a single brake light. The officer's mistake in interpreting the North Carolina statute was objectively reasonable because the language in the statute was ambiguous, the Court said, in an 8-1 ruling. Justice Sonia Sotomayor filed the lone dissent.

8. *Whren v. United States*, 517 U.S. 806 (1996). In a unanimous decision penned by Justice Antonin Scalia, the High Court ruled that the temporary detention of a motorist upon probable cause to believe that he committed a minor traffic infraction does not violate the Fourth Amendment's prohibition against unreasonable

seizures, even if a reasonable officer would not have stopped the motorist absent some additional law enforcement purpose.

9. *Chimel v. California*, 395 U.S. 752 (1969). *Chimel* holds that a search incident to a valid arrest must be limited to the arrestee's person and the area within his immediate control. Thus, officers lacking a search warrant were not authorized to conduct a search beyond the room in which Chimel was arrested.

The search-incident-to-arrest rule is recognized as an exception to the Fourth Amendment's search warrant requirement. The Court provided two justifications for this limited exception: 1) the need to ensure officer safety by removing any weapons that the arrestee might use in resisting arrest or escaping; and 2) preventing the arrestee from concealing or destroying evidence.

10. *United States v. Robinson*, 414 U.S. 218 (1973). In *Robinson*, the Court applied the *Chimel* analysis in the context of a search of the arrestee's person. *Robinson* holds that, in the case of a lawful custodial arrest, a full search of the person "incident to the arrest" is not only an exception to the warrant requirement of the Fourth Amendment, it is also a "reasonable" search under that Amendment. The fact that the arrest was made for a traffic offense, and it is not reasonable to assume that evidence of such an offense may be found on his person, does not preclude officers from conducting the search.

Justice Thurgood Marshall filed a dissenting opinion, joined by Justices William O. Douglas and William J. Brennan, Jr. Justice Marshall made the point that, since it is usually discretionary with the police officer whether to simply issue a citation rather than making an arrest for a traffic violation, police officers may be tempted to use a traffic arrest as a pretext in order to justify conducting a search.

Marshall argued that the majority opinion in *Robinson* departs from the rationale in *Terry v. Ohio* that a search must be reasonably related in scope to the circumstances that justified the interference in the first place. Removal of the cigarette package from Robinson's pocket exceeded the scope of a lawful search incident to arrest of a traffic violator, he concluded, and therefore should not fall under the search-incident-to-arrest exception to the Fourth Amendment's warrant requirement.

11. *Arizona v. Gant*, 556 U.S. 332 (2009). The Court's search-incident-to-arrest analysis culminates with *Gant*, which considered searches of an arrestee's vehicle. *Gant* holds that police may search a vehicle incident to a recent occupant's arrest only if the arrestee is within reaching distance of the passenger compartment at the time of the search or it is reasonable to believe the vehicle contains evidence of the offense for which the person was arrested. So in the case of an arrest for a traffic-related offense, police are not permitted to search the vehicle without a search warrant. As precedent for the decision in *Gant*, the Court cited the case of *Chimel v. California*, discussed in note 9 above.

Justice John Paul Stevens delivered the opinion of the Court in *Gant*, a 5-4 decision. Justices Stephen Breyer, Samuel Alito, John G. Roberts, Jr., and Anthony Kennedy dissented.

12. *Missouri v. McNeely*, 133 S.Ct. 1552 (2013). "BAC" refers to blood-alcohol concentration. Justice Sonia Sotomayor wrote the opinion in this 8-1 decision requiring the officer to obtain a warrant for the motorist's blood draw. The opinion stresses that the majority of states nowadays allow police to apply for search warrants remotely through means such as email and video conferencing.

The opinion distinguishes a 1966 case, *Schmerber v. California*, 384 U.S. 757 (1966), which upheld a warrantless blood test because, under the totality of circumstances in that case, there appeared to be an emergency. However, *McNeely* holds that, in drunk-driving investigations, the natural dissipation of alcohol in the bloodstream does not automatically constitute an exigency in every case sufficient to justify conducting a blood test without a warrant.

13. *Maryland v. King*, 133 S.Ct. 1958 (2013). A narrow majority of five Justices ruled that, where there is a valid arrest for a serious crime supported by probable cause, the suspect's Fourth Amendment expectation of privacy is not violated by the minor intrusion of a cheek swab to be tested for DNA. DNA identification of arrestees is deemed a "reasonable search" that can be done as part of a routine booking procedure. Justice Anthony Kennedy penned the majority opinion.

However, a vocal four-Member minority dissented, arguing that the practice of swabbing the cheeks of arrestees constitutes a suspicionless search that violates the Fourth Amendment in no uncertain terms. Justice Antonin Scalia wrote the opinion on behalf of the dissenting Justices.

14. *Birchfield v. North Dakota*, 579 U.S. ___ (2016). A 5-Justice majority held that the Fourth Amendment permits warrantless breath tests incident to arrests for drunk driving, but not warrantless blood tests. Justice Alito, writing on behalf of the majority, argued that requiring a warrant for breath tests would swamp the courts with a barrage of warrant applications. Justice Sotomayor, in a dissent joined by Justice Ginsburg, argued that statistics do not bear that out. Justice Thomas wrote separately, contending that neither blood nor breath testing incident to a valid drunk driving arrest should require a warrant. Due to Justice Scalia's death, only 8 Justices participated in the decision.

15. *Pennsylvania v. Mimms*, 434 U.S. 106 (1977). In a mere three-page opinion, a 6-Member majority of U.S. Supreme Court Justices extended the rationale of *Terry v. Ohio* by holding that, when a driver is stopped for a minor traffic violation, an officer may order a driver to exit his vehicle. Officers are authorized to take this action even where there is nothing to indicate that the driver is involved in any criminal activity.

Three dissenting Justices declared that the majority's decision "appears to abandon the central teaching of this Court's Fourth Amendment jurisprudence, which has ordinarily required individualized inquiry into the particular facts justifying every police intrusion".

16. *Brown v. Texas*, 443 U.S. 47 (1979). In a unanimous opinion, the High Court held that the Texas law making it a criminal act to refuse to give one's name and address to an officer violates the Fourth Amendment when the officer lacked any reasonable suspicion to believe that the target was engaged in or had engaged in criminal conduct.

The reasonableness of seizures that are less intrusive than a traditional arrest depends on a balance between the public's interest and the individual's right to personal security free from arbitrary interference by law officers, the Court said.

17. *Hiibel v. Nevada*, 542 U.S. 177 (2004). A divided Court, in a 5-4 decision, upheld the constitutionality of a Nevada law providing that a person is required to identify himself if stopped by a law enforcement officer under circumstances that reasonably indicate that the person has committed, is committing or is about to commit a crime. The requirement of reasonable suspicion is what differentiates the Nevada law from the Texas law discussed in the preceding note.

18. *United States v. Mendenhall*, 446 U.S. 544 (1980). This is a case where the Government conceded that its agents had neither a warrant nor probable cause to believe that the suspect was carrying narcotics. In a sharply divided decision, the High Court held that Sylvia Mendenhall's Fourth Amendment rights were not violated when she accompanied DEA agents from the concourse to the DEA office, and that her consent to the search of her person at the DEA office was therefore given voluntarily.

The *Mendenhall* opinion formulated a rule that a suspect is "seized" for Fourth Amendment purposes during an investigative stop only if, in view of all circumstances surrounding the incident, a reasonable person would have believed he or she was "not free to leave" and terminate the encounter.

However, a factually similar case, *Florida v. Royer*, 460 U.S. 491 (1983), went the other way. The Court held that Mark Royer, a nervous young man in an airport, was being illegally detained in a small room when he consented to a detective's search of his luggage. The Court concluded that the drugs found in the search of his luggage should be excluded from evidence because his consent was tainted by the illegality of his detention.

The outcome in these drug courier cases is highly dependent on the specific circumstances surrounding each incident. One factual difference between *Royer* and *Mendenhall* is that agents returned Mendenhall's driver's license and airplane ticket to her, whereas they held onto Royer's papers when they asked him to accompany them to their office. Another difference is that detectives retrieved Royer's luggage from the airline without his consent and brought it to the detectives' office to be searched. In Mendenhall's case, the drugs were on her person.

In *Royer*, the Court declined to establish a litmus paper test for distinguishing a consensual encounter from a seizure or for determining when a seizure exceeds the bounds of a *Terry*-type investigative stop.

19. *Florida v. Bostick*, 501 U.S. 429 (1991). In a 6-3 decision, the Court held that the Fourth Amendment is not violated when police board a bus, ask questions of an individual, and request consent to search the person's luggage, as long as officers do not convey a message that compliance with their requests is required.

This holding undercuts the "not free to leave" rubric enunciated in *Mendenhall*, since passengers sitting on a bus getting ready to leave a depot differ from persons walking around airports in that they can't simply walk away and thereby terminate the encounter.

Dissenting Justices compared the suspicionless sweep of buses to a dragnet, and argued that the practice violates the core values of the Fourth Amendment.

20. *Michigan Department of State Police v. Sitz*, 496 U.S. 444 (1990). In *Sitz*, the High Court held that a state's use of a program allowing brief stops at highway sobriety checkpoints, subject to carefully drawn guidelines, did not violate the Fourth Amendment. Such seizures are "reasonable," the Court said, because the intrusion is very slight when balanced against the benefit to the public. The Justices split 6-3.

21. *Indianapolis v. Edmond*, 531 U.S. 32 (2000). The U.S. Supreme Court held that, because the primary purpose of the Indianapolis drug interdiction checkpoint program is crime control, the checkpoints violate the Fourth Amendment. Justice Sandra Day O'Connor wrote the opinion on behalf of the majority. Chief Justice William Rehnquist dissented, along with Justices Antonin Scalia and Clarence Thomas.

22. *Illinois v. Gates*, 462 U.S. 213 (1983). In a 6-3 decision approving a judge's issuance of a search warrant, the High Court held that a "totality of

circumstances" test should be applied when evaluating the affidavit submitted in support of an application for a search warrant. In this case, the Court found that the affidavit detailing how police verified an anonymous tip sufficed to meet the test of probable cause required in the Fourth Amendment to the U.S. Constitution.

The *Gates* decision, written by Chief Justice William Rehnquist, abandoned the two-pronged test for probable cause that had been established under Chief Justice Earl Warren's tenure in *Aguilar v. Texas*, 378 U.S. 108 (1964) and *Spinelli v. United States*, 393 U.S. 410 (1969). Those cases stood for the proposition that a warrant application based on a tip from an anonymous informant must contain: 1) information regarding the source of the informant's knowledge, and 2) information demonstrating that he is truthful or reliable.

23. *Wong Sun v. United States*, 371 U.S. 471 (1963). The Court in *Wong Sun* acknowledged that Wong Sun's confession would ordinarily be deemed tainted by the fact that he was arrested without probable cause. But the Court decided to allow the confession to be admitted in this case because Wong Sun gave his confession several days after the unlawful arrest, when he voluntarily returned to the police station. The Court held that this delay broke the chain of causation, and dissipated the taint. Therefore, the confession was admissible in evidence against Wong Sun.

24. *United States v. Leon*, 468 U.S. 897 (1984). Justice Byron White penned the Court's opinion on behalf of a 6-Member majority. *Leon* holds that the Fourth Amendment Exclusionary Rule should not be applied so as to bar the use in the prosecution's case in chief of evidence obtained by officers acting in "good-faith" reliance on a search warrant issued by a judge, even when the warrant is later found to be defective. He wrote, "We have concluded that, in the Fourth amendment context, the Exclusionary Rule can be

modified somewhat without jeopardizing its ability to perform its intended functions."

But Justice Harry Blackmun, in a separate concurring opinion, expressed the caveat that "any empirical judgment about the effect of the Exclusionary Rule in a particular class of cases necessarily is a provisional one.... [T]he assumptions on which we proceed today cannot be cast in stone.... If it should emerge from experience that ... the good-faith exception to the exclusionary rule results in a material change in police compliance with the Fourth Amendment, we shall have to reconsider ...."

Justices William J. Brennan, Jr., Thurgood Marshall, and John Paul Stevens dissented. Justice Brennan's dissenting opinion argues that, "the language of deterrence and of cost/benefit analysis, if used indiscriminately, can have a narcotic effect."

Application of the cost-benefit-analysis rationale employed in *Leon*, combined with the attenuation doctrine relied on in *Wong Sun*, led to a bizarre result in a case called *Utah v. Strieff*, 579 U.S. ___ (2016). A police detective saw a man exit a Salt Lake City house that police suspected, based on an anonymous tip, of being a drug house. After the man walked to a nearby convenience store, the detective, despite the lack of any facts that qualified as reasonable suspicion, demanded the man's identification. The detective then relayed the information to a police dispatcher, and learned that the man had an outstanding warrant for an unpaid parking ticket. Based on the outstanding warrant, the detective arrested the man and searched him incident to the arrest, finding a baggie of meth on his person.

In a 5-3 decision, the *Strieff* Court held that the evidence discovered on the man's person was admissible because the unlawful stop was sufficiently attenuated by the pre-existing arrest warrant. "The outstanding arrest warrant for Strieff's arrest is a critical intervening circumstance," the Court said. Justice Sotomayor, in dissent, complained that unlawful suspicionless stops like the one in *Strieff* "corrode all our civil liberties and threaten all our lives."

25. *Herring v. United States*, 555 U.S. 135 (2009). The 5-Member majority in this closely divided case held that "when police mistakes are the result of negligence such as that described here, rather than systematic error or reckless disregard of constitutional requirements, any marginal deterrence [gained by exclusion of tainted evidence] does not 'pay its way'."

Speaking on behalf of the minority, Justice Ruth Bader Ginsburg argued that the Exclusionary Rule is, for all practical purposes, the only means of redress available for most people whose rights have been violated. Ginsburg pointed out that the warrant clerk admitted in testimony that she'd had problems with communicating about warrants several times before.

Ginsburg noted that electronic databases form the nervous system of contemporary criminal justice operations. Accordingly, the sanction of suppressing tainted evidence is needed to deter police agencies from neglecting to monitor their databases, she said.

26. *Florida v. Jardines*, 133 S.Ct. 1409 (2013). In a 5-4 opinion, the U.S. Supreme Court held that the Government's warrantless use of a drug-sniffing dog to investigate the contents of one's home and its immediate surroundings constituted an unreasonable search in violation of the Fourth Amendment. Justice Scalia, writing on behalf of the majority, stated that, "when it comes to the Fourth Amendment, the home is first among equals."

Note that, under the holding in *Illinois v. Gates* (see note 22 above), police could not have obtained a warrant on the basis of the original informant's tip, because a tip that has not been verified before conducting a search is insufficient to provide the probable cause needed to obtain a search warrant.

Justice Antonin Scalia's opinion harkens back to the old English common law notion of physical trespass to property, a concept that pre-dated America's Fourth Amendment. Justice Elena Kagan, in a concurring opinion joined by Justices Ruth Bader Ginsburg and Sonia Sotomayor, states that she would have preferred to base the decision on the homeowner's reasonable expectation of privacy. This interpretation of the Fourth Amendment was articulated by the High Court in *Katz v. United States*, 389 U.S. 347 (1967). (See note 4 above.)

27. The U.S. Supreme Court had held, in two prior cases, that visual surveillance of private homes from the air did not constitute a search for Fourth Amendment purposes because the aerial inspection involved no physical invasion, and the marijuana was visible with the naked eye. (*California v. Ciraolo*, 476 U.S. 207 (1986), and *Florida v. Riley*, 488 U.S. 445 (1989).) However, the Court was sharply divided in both cases.

Riley concerned the constitutionality of a flyover at 400 feet by a police helicopter to spy on Riley's greenhouse. Justice John Paul Stevens' dissenting opinion quotes several prior high court decisions for the proposition that protecting one's privacy from arbitrary intrusion by police is at the core of the Fourth Amendment. He compares the aerial surveillance in *Riley* to the Police Patrol's snooping in George Orwell's classic novel, *Nineteen Eighty-Four*.

28. *Kyllo v. United States*, 533 U.S. 27 (2001). In a 5-4 decision, the Court held that where the Government uses a device that is not in general public use to explore details inside a private home, the surveillance constitutes a Fourth Amendment "search," and is presumptively unreasonable without a warrant. Justice Antonin Scalia wrote the majority opinion, while Justice John Paul Stevens penned the dissent.

29. *United States v. Antoine Jones*, 132 S.Ct. 945 (2012). Justice Antonin Scalia, who penned the decision on behalf of a unanimous Court, wrote that when the officers physically attached the GPS device to monitor the vehicle's movements, their actions qualified as a warrantless "search," and therefore violated the Fourth Amendment.

Five of the nine Justices, in two concurring opinions, objected to limiting the decision to cases involving *physical* intrusions on property. Citing *Katz v. United States*, they pointed out that the opinion fails to address GPS tracking by means that do not involve physical contact. Some of the concurring Members also objected to Justice Scalia's failure to consider one of the factors relied on in *Katz, i.e.*, whether the defendant's reasonable expectation of privacy was violated by the long-term monitoring.

Justice Scalia's opinion declines to say whether he would have found the monitoring to be unconstitutional if there was no physical trespass to property. He states: "It may be that achieving the same result through electronic means, without an accompanying trespass, is an unconstitutional invasion of privacy, but the present case does not require us to answer that question."

30. *David L. Riley v. California* and *United States v. Brima Wurie*, 134 S.Ct. 2473 (2014). These two cases, decided in a single opinion, hold that police are required to obtain a search warrant before proceeding to search digital information on a cell phone seized from a person who has been arrested.

Riley concerns a driver pulled over in San Diego, California for expired license tags. In the course of the stop, the officer discovered that Riley's driver's license had been suspended, and he placed Riley under arrest. Incident to the arrest, the officer searched Riley's person, and found Riley's smart phone as well as items associated with the "Bloods" street gang. Subsequent warrantless searches of the smart phone disclosed links to the "Crip Killers" and to a gang-related shooting.

Wurie concerns police surveillance of an apparent drug sale that resulted in Wurie's arrest. Officers seized two cell phones from Wurie's person. A subsequent warrantless search-incident-to-arrest of one of Wurie's phones led officers to his home. After obtaining a warrant to search his home, officers seized a large stash of crack cocaine from the residence.

In each of these cases, defense counsel argued that all of the evidence obtained, directly or indirectly, from the cell phone search, should be suppressed as the fruit of an unconstitutional search of the cell phone.

Chief Justice John G. Roberts, Jr. wrote the opinion on behalf of a unanimous Court. Roberts elaborated at length on why digital devices, with their vast stores of personal data, should be treated differently from physical objects such as guns or cigarette packs.

31. *Illinois v. Caballes*, 543 U.S. 405 (2005). *Caballes* is a good example of how differently the Court views searches involving vehicles as opposed to residences. Justice Stevens, writing on behalf of a 6-member majority, ruled that, because a dog sniff of a vehicle does not compromise any legitimate interest in privacy, the dog sniff should not be deemed a "search" subject to the Fourth Amendment. The dog sniff was therefore permissible, given the fact that the original traffic stop was lawful, and the driver's detention was not prolonged beyond the time reasonably required to complete the mission of issuing a warning ticket.

Justice Ruth Bader Ginsburg, joined by Justice David Souter, filed a dissenting opinion, arguing that police violated Caballes' Fourth Amendment rights when, without cause to suspect wrongdoing, they conducted a dog sniff of his vehicle. Justice William Rehnquist took no part in the decision of the case.

32. *Rodriguez v. United States*, 135 S.Ct. 1609 (2015). Justice Ginsburg wrote the majority opinion in this 6-3 decision. The Court held that, absent reasonable suspicion that a driver has committed a crime other than a traffic violation, prolonging a traffic stop in order to conduct a dog sniff violates the Fourth Amendment's ban on unreasonable searches and seizures. (Note that, in *Caballes*, the dog sniff took place before the traffic cop had finished writing up the traffic stop. In that case, the sniff was initiated by another officer who rushed to the scene on his own initiative.)

The majority's opinion points out that the trial court found detention for the dog sniff in *Rodriguez* was not supported by reasonable suspicion on the part of the officer. Moreover, the appeals court did not disturb the trial magistrate's determination that the officer lacked reasonable suspicion.

Justices Alito and Thomas, in separate dissenting opinions, emphasize the officer's testimony before the trial court in which he alleged that he smelled air freshener in the vehicle, and suspected it was being used to mask the presence of drugs. Alito and Thomas argue that the officer's inference sufficed to give him reasonable suspicion of a drug crime. In joining Justice Thomas' dissent, Justice Kennedy distances himself from the portion of Justice Thomas' opinion that speculated on whether the officer had reasonable suspicion of drug possession, preferring to allow the appeals court to make that determination.

33. *Schneckloth v. Bustamonte*, 412 U.S. 218 (1973). The question in this case is whether consent to the search of a vehicle was "voluntary" in light of the fact that consent was given in a coercive atmosphere, and police did not advise the person that he had a right to withhold consent.

A majority of the Justices held that where the subject of a search is not in custody at the time his consent is requested, his consent will be deemed voluntary so long as the consent was not the result of duress or coercion, express or implied. Police are not required to advise the subject of his right to withhold consent. Justices William O. Douglas, William J. Brennan, Jr., and Thurgood Marshall filed separate dissenting opinions.

34. *Rakas v. Illinois*, 439 U.S. 128 (1978). In a 5-4 decision, the U.S. Supreme Court held that passengers who asserted neither a property nor a possessory interest in the automobile searched had no right to mount a Fourth Amendment challenge to the search of the passenger compartment.

35. *Maryland v. Jerry Lee Wilson*, 519 U.S. 408 (1997). In a 7-2 decision, the Court held that an officer making a traffic stop may order passengers to exit the car pending completion of the stop.

36. See *Rakas v. Illinois*, in note 34 above.

37. *Brendlin v. California*, 551 U.S. 249 (2007). When police make a traffic stop, a passenger in the car, like the driver, is seized for Fourth Amendment purposes and so may challenge the stop's constitutionality. The decision was unanimous.

38. See *Maryland v. Jerry Lee Wilson*, in note 35 above.

39. *Arizona v. Lemon Johnson*, 555 U.S. 323 (2009). An officer's pat-down of a passenger in the course of a lawful traffic stop does not violate the Fourth Amendment's ban on unreasonable searches and seizures, notwithstanding the fact that the officer lacked a reasonable belief that the passenger was involved in criminal activity. However, to be lawful, police must harbor a reasonable suspicion that the person subjected to the frisk is armed and dangerous. The decision was unanimous.

40. *Bailey v. United States*, 133 S.Ct. 1031 (2013). Law enforcement officers are not permitted to detain a person incident to the execution of a search warrant if the person is outside the immediate vicinity of where the search was to be conducted. In short, there is a "spatial dimension" to detentions of persons conducted incident to a lawful search.

The majority opinion, written by Justice Anthony Kennedy, expressly declines to define the term "immediate vicinity." In an earlier decision, *Michigan v. Summers*, 452 U.S. 692 (1981), the Court permitted police armed with a search warrant to detain individuals who were standing right outside the residence to be searched.

41. *Georgia v. Randolph*, 547 U.S. 103 (2006). In this hotly contested decision, the U.S. Supreme Court held that a physically present co-occupant's stated refusal to permit entry renders a warrantless entry and search unreasonable and invalid for purposes of the Fourth Amendment.

42. *Fernandez v. California*, 134 S.Ct. 1126 (2014). A six-Member majority held that, if one resident refuses to allow police to search his residence without a search warrant, police may lawfully search the residence if another resident consents to the search once the objecting resident is no longer physically present. This ruling applies even if the police forcefully remove the objecting occupant, provided that police acted lawfully in removing him from the residence.

Three Justices, in an opinion penned by Justice Ruth Bader Ginsburg and joined by Justices Sonia Sotomayor and Elena Kagan, dissented. They argued that this result is directly contrary to the Court's decision in *Georgia v. Randolph* (note 41). In that case, Mrs. Randolph called police to the family home to complain that her husband was a cocaine user. Mr. Randolph refused the officer's request to search the home, but the wife consented. The *Randolph* Court held that Mrs. Randolph's consent was insufficient to justify the warrantless search, and that the evidence found in the warrantless search had to be excluded from trial.

The majority's opinion in *Fernandez* explains the discrepancy by saying that, in *Randolph*, the objecting resident was physically present when the search was conducted, whereas in the case of Mr. Fernandez, he was no longer at the scene when police asked for the cotenant's consent.

During oral argument of *Fernandez* in the U.S. Supreme Court, some of the Justices asked whether this case means that police will never need a warrant if all they have to do is arrest and remove people who refuse to give police total control. Justice Sotomayor quipped that all couples preparing to wed should include some protective language in a prenuptial agreement to prevent joint access to personal possessions.

43. *Camara v. Municipal Court of the City and County of San Francisco*, 387 U.S. 523 (1967). The High Court held that the Fourth Amendment gives one a constitutional right to insist that inspectors obtain a search warrant in order to conduct a code enforcement inspection of the person's personal residence. Additional discussion of *Camara* is contained in its companion case, *See v. City of Seattle*, 387 U.S. 541 (1967).

III. Turning the Tables

1. *Bivens v. Six Unknown Federal Narcotics Agents*, 403 U.S. 388 (1971). The question in *Bivens* was whether the Fourth Amendment authorizes a private lawsuit for damages caused by an unreasonable search and seizure. The High Court held that a person whose Fourth Amendment rights are violated by federal drug agents is entitled to recover money damages for any injuries he has suffered as a result of said violation.

The question of immunity for the agents was not addressed in this case, since the court below had not ruled on it.

2. In *Monell v. Department of Social Services of the City of New York*, 436 U.S. 658 (1978), the U.S. Supreme Court held that both local governing bodies and local officials can be sued directly under the federal Civil Rights Act for monetary relief where the officials allegedly violated the plaintiff's constitutional rights. Consequently, those claiming to be injured by police misconduct were able, for the first time, to reach into the deep pockets of municipalities.

Monell went farther than a prior High Court decision, *Monroe v. Pape*, 365 U.S. 167 (1961), which acknowledged that individuals are allowed to sue local police officers, but held that municipal corporations cannot be sued under the federal Civil Rights Act for the actions of their agents. *Monroe* involved a particularly egregious home invasion and arrest executed by thirteen Chicago police officers.

3. The American legal system gives absolute immunity to prosecutors against claims of malicious prosecution when they ask a grand jury to indict a suspect. However, absolute immunity is limited to functions intimately associated with the judicial component of the criminal justice system, and does not extend to police.

The United States Supreme Court has found that the lesser protection of "qualified immunity" provides ample protections for law enforcement officers. The doctrine of qualified immunity protects government officials from liability for civil damages.

Malley v. Briggs, 475 U.S. 335 (1986), held that a law enforcement officer will be shielded by qualified immunity for submitting a faulty warrant application unless the application is so lacking in indicia of probable cause that no reasonable officer could have believed it complied with the Fourth Amendment. Qualified immunity gives police breathing room to make reasonable but mistaken judgments.

4. *Pearson v. Callahan*, 555 U.S. 223 (2009). *Callahan* holds that, even where police officers violate a person's Fourth Amendment rights, they are entitled to qualified immunity if the action they took did not violate a rule that was "clearly established" at the time the events took place. The decision was unanimous.

This case involved a drug sting operation where the target's daughter let the informant into the target's residence to purchase drugs from her father. After the informant signaled that the sale was complete, police entered and searched the residence. Police had no search or arrest warrants.

The Court declined to decide the question of whether the search passed constitutional muster. Instead, the Justices opted to eliminate the need to answer that question by deciding that the law violated by the officers was not "clearly established" at the time of the raid.

The raid took place in 2002. It was not until 2006 that the High Court decided *Georgia v. Randolph* (see Chapter II, note 41), which is at odds with the "consent-once-removed" doctrine. The "consent-once-removed" doctrine permitted a warrantless entry by police officers into a home when consent to enter has already been granted to an undercover officer or informant who has discovered contraband in plain view.

5. *Tennessee v. Garner*, 471 U.S. 1 (1985). In a 6-3 opinion, the Court held that the Tennessee statute permitting police to use deadly force to arrest a fleeing suspect is unconstitutional unless police have probable cause to believe that the suspect poses a significant threat of death or serious physical injury to police or others.

6. *Dethorne Graham v. Connor*, 490 U.S. 386 (1989). Dethorne Graham filed his excessive force lawsuit in

federal court, seeking monetary damages under the federal Civil Rights Act.

In a unanimous opinion, the U.S. Supreme Court decided that all claims of use of excessive force by law enforcement officers must be analyzed using the Fourth Amendment's "objective reasonableness" standard. "Determining whether the force used to effect a particular seizure is 'reasonable' under the Fourth Amendment requires a careful balancing of the nature and quality of the intrusion on the individual's Fourth Amendment interests against the countervailing governmental interests at stake," the Court said.

7. The High Court spoke with one voice in *Tolan v. Cotton*, 134 S.Ct. 1861 (2014), indicating that this civil rights claim for use of excessive force should not be summarily dismissed, as genuine issues of material fact existed that must be resolved by a jury. Justice Samuel Alito, concurring in the judgment, pointed out that the issue in the case was whether the relevant evidence, viewed in the light most favorable to the plaintiffs, is sufficient to support a decision in their favor. The lower courts should not have dismissed the lawsuit before a jury had an opportunity to weigh the evidence.

8. In *Plumhoff v. Rickard*, 134 S.Ct. 2012 (2014), a unanimous Court agreed that the civil rights lawsuit filed by the driver's daughter alleging use of excessive force should be dismissed because the Court could find no "clearly established law" on the books forbidding the police to fire into the car under these circumstances. Therefore, police were entitled to qualified immunity.

A majority also agreed that police did not violate the Fourth Amendment when they fired shots into the car in order to end a serious threat to public safety. Justices Stephen Breyer and Ruth Bader Ginsburg disagreed with the latter proposition, but did not explain the basis for their disagreement concerning the alleged violation of Rickard's constitutional rights.

In a prior case, *Scott v. Harris*, 550 U.S. 372 (2007), Justice John Paul Stevens had quoted the Georgia Association of Chiefs of Police for the proposition that "Pursuits should usually be discontinued when the violator's identity has been established to the point that later apprehension can be accomplished without danger to the public."

Nonetheless, in 2015, the High Court, in a subsequent high-speed police chase decision, noted that the Court has never found the use of deadly force by police in connection with a dangerous car chase to violate the Fourth Amendment. (See *Mullenix v. Luna*, 577 U.S. ___ (2015).) Moreover, qualified immunity protects police actions in the "hazy border" between excessive and acceptable force, the Court said.

9. *Ryburn v. Huff*, 132 S.Ct. 987 (2012). All nine Justices agreed that the Fourth Amendment permits law enforcement officers to enter a home without a warrant where there is an objectively reasonable basis for fearing that violence is imminent. However, note that the officers in this case did not conduct any search of the persons or property in the house -- their intrusion was limited to a verbal Q and A exchange.

The facts in *Huff* differ substantially from those in *Mapp v. Ohio*, discussed in Chapter 2, note 3. In *Mapp*, police had several hours that could have been used to obtain a search warrant, and the officers in *Mapp* rummaged through the entire dwelling.

10. *Atwater v. City of Lago Vista*, 532 U.S. 318 (2001). Under Texas law, failure to secure seatbelts carried a fine of $25 to $50. After Ms. Atwater paid a $50 fine, she and her husband filed a civil rights lawsuit alleging that the city had violated her Fourth Amendment right to be free from unreasonable seizure.

In a 5-4 decision, the Court held that the Fourth Amendment does not forbid a warrantless arrest for a minor criminal offense, such as a seatbelt violation punishable only by a fine.

    Justice Sandra Day O'Connor, writing on behalf of a 4-Member minority, argued that, where history is inconclusive, the Court should have followed the normal practice of evaluating a search or seizure under traditional standards of reasonableness. There was nothing reasonable about the severe intrusion on Ms. Atwater's liberty caused by a full custodial arrest, she said, since even the majority had conceded that the arrest was a "pointless indignity."

11. *Ontario v. Quon*, 560 U.S. 746 (2010). *Quon* holds that, where the Government's search of a police officer's city-owned pager was "reasonable" in that it was conducted for a legitimate work-related purpose, and where it was not excessive in scope, the search did not violate the Fourth Amendment's ban on "unreasonable searches and seizures." The vote of the Justices was unanimous.

12. *Safford Unified School District #1 v. Redding*, 557 U.S. 364 (2009). *Safford* holds that searches of students conducted by school officials are governed by a Fourth Amendment standard of reasonable suspicion. A school search is permissible in its scope when the measures adopted are reasonably related to the objectives of the search and not excessively intrusive in light of the age and sex of the student and the nature of the infraction. Therefore, subjecting a 13-year-old female student to a strip search violates the Fourth Amendment where it is based on a groundless suspicion that she might be hiding medicine in her underwear.

    However, the Court ruled that officials were protected from liability by qualified immunity because there was no clearly established precedent showing that the search violated the Fourth Amendment.

13. *Florence v. County of Burlington*, 132 S.Ct. 1510 (2012). In a 5-4 decision, the United States Supreme Court held that the Fourth and Fourteenth Amendments do not bar jail officials from conducting visual strip searches of detainees arrested for minor offenses where they are to be admitted to the general jail population, as long as the searches do not involve physical contact by corrections officers. The legitimacy of the search is due to the need for jail officials to ensure jail security, the Court said. The Court reserved judgment on the legality of a suspicionless strip search in minor offenses where the arrestee will be kept segregated from the general jail population pending the arrestee's release.

Four dissenting Justices pointed out that the majority of federal appeals courts have ruled that suspicionless strip-searches are prohibited in the case of minor offenses that do not involve drugs or violence.

14. *Messerschmidt v. Millender*, 132 S.Ct. 1235 (2012). The *Millender* Court held that the officers were entitled to qualified immunity because the warrant in this case was not so obviously defective that no reasonable officer could have believed it to be valid. The majority reasoned that, under the facts of this case, an officer could reasonably have believed the scope of the warrant to be supported by probable cause.

Dissenting Justices argued that the warrant in *Millender* resembled the "general warrants" that the Framers sought to prevent when they drafted the Fourth Amendment. In the minds of the dissenters, the broad warrant issued here clearly violated the Fourth Amendment.

IV. Representation, Self-Incrimination, and Identification

1. In 1938, the U.S. Supreme Court decided for the first time that the Sixth Amendment to the United States Constitution required counsel to be provided in all

federal court prosecutions for defendants who are financially unable to retain counsel. *Johnson v. Zerbst*, 304 U.S. 458 (1938). However, the case did not address the provision of counsel for those prosecuted in state courts.

2. *Betts v. Brady*, 316 U.S. 455 (1942), and its progeny.

3. Anthony Lewis, Gideon's Trumpet, Random House: New York, 1964, at p. 10.

4. *Amicus curiae* is a Latin term meaning "friend of the court." *Amicus curiae* briefs may, under certain circumstances, be submitted by those who are not parties to the lawsuit in order to provide additional information that may assist the Court in making a proper decision.

5. *Gideon v. Wainwright*, 372 U.S. 335 (1963). In a unanimous decision, the U.S. Supreme Court found that, "in our adversary system of criminal justice, any person haled into court, who is too poor to hire a lawyer, cannot be assured a fair trial unless counsel is provided for him." Thus, the Court held that every person accused of a crime, whether state or federal, is entitled to a lawyer at trial. Gideon was tried for a felony (a serious crime, usually punishable by at least one year in prison or death), and the Court abstained from elaborating on whether its ruling applied where the person is accused of a lesser offense.

The *Gideon* decision overruled the High Court's 1942 decision in *Betts v. Brady*, 316 U.S. 455 (1942). *Betts* had held that defendants tried for felonies in state courts are not deprived of the due process guaranteed by the Fourteenth Amendment because of the trial judge's refusal to appoint counsel for the accused, since the Due Process Clause of the Fourteenth Amendment does not incorporate the guarantees found in the Sixth Amendment, and appointment of counsel is not a fundamental right essential to a fair trial.

While the *Gideon* Court held that the right to counsel must be recognized as a fundamental right embraced by the Fourteenth Amendment, the Court stopped short of explicitly stating that the Fourteenth Amendment "incorporates" the Sixth Amendment as such.

6. *Escobedo v. Illinois*, 378 U.S. 478 (1964). In a 5-4 decision, the U.S. Supreme Court held that where a suspect has been taken into police custody and interrogated after having requested and been denied the opportunity to consult with his lawyer, and police have not effectively warned him of his constitutional right to remain silent, that constitutes a denial of counsel in violation of the Sixth Amendment. The Court also held that the constitutional violation prohibits the prosecution from using at trial any incriminating statement elicited by police during the tainted interrogation.

Note that, while the Court in *Gideon* stopped short of holding that the Sixth Amendment right to counsel applies to those tried in state courts, the Court in *Escobedo* went a step further by stating that denying the accused access to his lawyer during an interrogation violates the Sixth Amendment to the Constitution made obligatory upon the states by the Fourteenth Amendment. Thus, the Court, for the first time, made it explicit that the Sixth Amendment right to counsel applies to state court trials.

The *Escobedo* case stands as an essential building block for the Court's decision in *Miranda v. Arizona*, decided just two years after *Escobedo*.

7. *Griffin v. California*, 380 U.S. 609 (1965), hinges on the High Court's decision in *Malloy v. Hogan*, 378 U.S. 1 (1964). *Malloy* held that persons prosecuted in state courts may avail themselves of the Fifth Amendment's privilege against compulsory self-incrimination. *Malloy* adopted the Warren Court's "incorporation doctrine," which said that the Fourteenth Amendment's Due

Process Clause incorporates certain rights contained in the first eight Amendments, and applies them to the states. Previously, those rights were considered the exclusive province of those prosecuted in the federal court system.

In the wake of *Malloy*, the High Court considered for the first time the question of whether state courts could permit prosecutors to comment on the fact that an accused had declined to take the witness stand in his own defense. In *Griffin*, the Court held that, since the Fifth Amendment's privilege against self-incrimination applies in state courts, state court prosecutors were forbidden to comment on the accused's silence, and judges were not permitted to instruct a jury that such silence can be deemed evidence of guilt. The Chief Justice took no part in *Griffin*, and two other Justices joined in filing a dissenting opinion. (Note that, when the Court refers to "state courts," the Justices mean the state court systems, which include local courts.)

8. *Miranda v. Arizona*, 384 U.S. 436 (1966). A razor-thin majority of five Justices led by Chief Justice Earl Warren found that, in light of the confusion following prior court rulings, such as *Escobedo v. Illinois* (see note 6 above), it was necessary to provide concrete constitutional guidelines for law enforcement agencies and courts to follow.

The majority in *Miranda* held that the prosecution may not use statements, whether exculpatory or inculpatory, stemming from custodial interrogation of a defendant unless it demonstrates the use of procedural safeguards effective to secure the privilege against self-incrimination. So prior to any questioning, the person must be warned that: 1) he has a right to remain silent; 2) that any statement he makes may be used as evidence against him; 3) that he has a right to the presence of an attorney; and 4) if he cannot afford an attorney one will be appointed for him prior to any questioning if he so desires.

Miranda remains the law today, although it has been somewhat eroded by decisions such as *New York v. Quarles*, 467 U.S. 649 (1984), which provides for a "public safety exception" that allows police to delay administering the warnings under exigent circumstances.

However, *Miranda* was reaffirmed in the year 2000 by none other than the ultra-conservative Chief Justice William Rehnquist. In *Dickerson v. United States*, 530 U.S. 428 (2000), he delivered the Court's opinion holding that *Miranda*, being a decision based on the Constitution, could not be overruled by an Act of Congress.

9. *Berghuis v. Thompkins*, 560 U.S. 370 (2010). Swing voter Anthony Kennedy wrote the opinion on behalf of a 5-4 majority. *Thompkins* held: a) In order to "invoke" his right to remain silent under the Fifth Amendment, a suspect's *Miranda* right to remain silent must be invoked unambiguously, for example, by stating that he did not want to talk. b) Thompkins waived his right to remain silent by making an uncoerced statement to police. c) Police were not required to obtain an express waiver of Thompkins' *Miranda* rights before commencing interrogation.

Justice Sonia Sotomayor filed a dissenting opinion joined by Justices John Paul Stevens, Ruth Bader Ginsburg, and Stephen Breyer. She wrote: "The Court concludes today that a criminal suspect waives his right to remain silent if, after sitting tacit and uncommunicative through nearly three hours of police interrogation, he utters a few one-word responses. The Court also concludes that a suspect who wishes to guard his right to remain silent against such a finding of 'waiver' must, counterintuitively, speak .... Both propositions mark a substantial retreat from the protection that *Miranda* ... has long provided during custodial interrogation."

Her opinion reminds readers that custodial interrogation is inherently coercive, which is why the prosecution ought to have the burden of proving that the suspect waived his *Miranda* rights. Shifting this burden to the defendant, she said, "turns *Miranda* upside down."

10. *Salinas v. Texas*, 133 S.Ct. 2174 (2013). According to the plurality's opinion, the Fifth Amendment does not bar a prosecutor from commenting during trial on an un-Mirandized pre-arrest suspect's failure to answer a question during interrogation unless the suspect expressly invokes the Fifth Amendment right in response to the officer's question.

Although Salinas was questioned at a police station, the Court did not deem him to be "in custody" because he came to the police station willingly. *Miranda* warnings are only required for those in the custody of police.

At oral argument, counsel for Salinas contended that it would be unfair to require a suspect unschooled in legal doctrine to do anything more than remain silent in order to invoke his privilege against self-incrimination.

The dissenting opinion argues that the holding of this case gives Salinas a Hobson's choice -- choosing between incrimination through speech and incrimination through silence. Justice Stephen Breyer, writing on behalf of the four dissenting Justices, asks: how can an individual who is not a lawyer know that the words "I invoke my Fifth Amendment privilege" are legally magic?

11. *J.D.B. v. North Carolina*, 131 S.Ct. 2394 (2011). In a 5-4 decision, the U.S. Supreme Court held that police must take a person's age into account when deciding whether a suspect is deemed to be "in custody," triggering the requirement to administer *Miranda* warnings before commencing questioning.

12. *Argersinger v. Hamlin*, 407 U.S. 25 (1972). The High Court held that a person who is unable to afford a lawyer has a Sixth Amendment right to court-appointed

counsel, whether the accused is tried in federal or state court, and whether he is accused of a felony or a lesser crime that results in the deprivation of liberty.

The *Argersinger* decision has been interpreted to mean that the right of an indigent accused to have counsel appointed is limited to cases where jail time is actually imposed, and not on whether the maximum penalty under the law for the offense charged authorizes jail time. This differs from the right-to-jury case discussed in Chapter V, *Duncan v. Louisiana*, where the right hinges on the maximum penalty allowed by law.

13. See Nancy Albert-Goldberg, *Los Angeles County Public Defender Office in Perspective*, 45 CAL. WESTERN LAW REV. 445 (2009), http://www.cwsl.edu.ws/albert-goldberg, for an analysis of the country's largest public defender system.

14. *Strickland v. Washington*, 466 U.S. 668 (1984). In an 8-1 decision, the High Court held that the Sixth Amendment right to counsel is the right to the effective assistance of counsel. A convicted defendant's claim that counsel's assistance was so defective as to require reversal of a conviction or setting aside a sentence requires that the defendant show: 1) that counsel's performance was so deficient that counsel was not functioning as the "counsel" guaranteed by the Sixth Amendment; and 2) that the deficient performance prejudiced the defense, such that counsel's errors were serious enough as to deprive the defendant of a fair trial.

Justice Marshall, in dissent, argued that the first prong of the majority's standard is too vague to provide useful guidance, while the "prejudice" prong is impractical and unworkable.

15. This set of verses concerns a pair of decisions that the United States Supreme Court handed down on the same day. Both cases raised questions about whether a

defendant has a Sixth Amendment right to the effective assistance of counsel in the plea bargaining process.

In *Lafler v. Cooper*, 132 S.Ct. 1376 (2012), defense counsel provided ineffective advice that led to defendant's rejecting a plea bargain in favor of proceeding to trial. The defendant proceeded to trial, was convicted, and received a far longer sentence than that contained in the original plea offer.

In *Missouri v. Frye*, 132 S.Ct. 1399 (2012), defense counsel provided ineffective assistance of counsel by failing to inform the client that a plea deal had been offered by the prosecution. As a result, the defendant later pled guilty on terms that were far less favorable than those initially offered.

The majority held, in *Cooper* and *Frye*, that defendants have a Sixth Amendment right to the effective assistance of counsel in plea bargaining, and that it was violated in each of these cases.

16. About eight months after deciding *Lafler v. Cooper*, the High Court handed down a unanimous decision showing that a defendant bears a heavy burden of proof when seeking a lower sentence on the ground that her lawyer was ineffective in advising her to go to trial rather than accept a plea deal. In *Sherry Burt, Warden, v. Vonlee Titlow*, 134 S.Ct. 10 (2013), the Court debated whether Vonlee Titlow's sentence of 20-to-40 years in prison for second-degree murder should be reversed due to her lawyer's ineffective assistance during the plea bargaining process.

Vonlee's first lawyer had negotiated a plea bargain for her whereby she would receive a sentence of 7-to-15 years in prison for manslaughter if she agreed to testify against her aunt at the aunt's murder trial. Vonlee allegedly assisted her Aunt Billie in killing Billie's alcoholic husband. Billie later paid Vonlee $100,000 in hush money. Vonlee did tell one person -- her boyfriend -- who then wore a wire for the police while she told the story.

Vonlee passed a polygraph denying planning to kill her uncle. Afterwards, she told a jailer that she was innocent. The jailer advised Vonlee to withdraw the plea and go to trial instead. Vonlee then hired a new lawyer named Toca, who demanded a lower minimum sentence (3 years instead of 7) in exchange for the guilty plea and testimony. But the prosecutor rejected the proposal, so Vonlee declined to testify against her aunt, and Toca withdrew Vonlee's guilty plea.

Toca failed to obtain Vonlee's file, inspect the government's discovery materials, or speak with her prior attorney until six weeks after recommending that she withdraw her guilty plea. After he finally reviewed the file, Toca withdrew as counsel. Vonlee then went to trial, represented by court-appointed counsel.

At her trial, Vonlee admitted to putting her hand over her uncle's mouth after Billie poured vodka down his throat, and confirmed that she had poured a small quantity as well, but ultimately stopped Billie from giving him more alcohol and then left the room. When she returned, she saw Billie holding a pillow over her uncle's face. The jury convicted her of second degree murder. The Michigan Court of Appeals affirmed Vonlee's sentence on appeal.

The U.S. Supreme Court ultimately declined to reverse the case for two reasons: 1) Federal courts give both the state court and the defense attorney the benefit of the doubt when it comes to making factual findings about the effectiveness of counsel; and 2) It was not objectively unreasonable to recommend that the defendant refrain from pleading guilty in a case where she had proclaimed her innocence.

17. In *Neil v. Biggers*, 409 U.S. 188 (1972), the U.S. Supreme Court laid down a set of factors to be applied in determining whether the eyewitness's identification was reliable.

18. *Barion Perry v. New Hampshire*, 132 S.Ct. 716 (2012). Prior cases had held that trial judges were required to screen eyewitness identifications for reliability prior to trial. If the screening showed a very substantial likelihood that the wrong person was identified, then the judge had to exclude the evidence at trial.

In an 8-1 decision, the *Perry* Court held that the Due Process Clause of the Fourteenth Amendment does not require trial judges to conduct preliminary assessments of the reliability of eyewitness identifications made under suggestive circumstances where the circumstances were not arranged by police. The majority opinion reasoned that the purpose of prior cases was to deter police from rigging eyewitness identifications.

Justice Sonia Sotomayor filed a dissenting opinion, arguing that the majority's decision would add to the country's serious epidemic of wrongful convictions. Studies show that eyewitness misidentification is the single greatest cause of wrongful convictions, she said.

V. Taking Aim at Gun Laws

1. In *Miller v. United States*, 307 U.S. 174 (1939), the High Court ruled on a case where the defendants were accused of violating the National Firearms Act by possessing a shotgun having a barrel of less than 18 inches in length. Defendants argued that the Act infringed on their Second Amendment right to keep and bear arms. In a unanimous opinion, the Court held that use or possession of a firearm that is not part of ordinary military equipment or that could contribute to the common defense is not guaranteed by the Second Amendment. Justice William O. Douglas took no part in the decision.

2. Justice Antonin Scalia, writing on behalf of a 5-4 majority in *District of Columbia v. Heller*, 554 U.S. 570 (2008), said that the District of Columbia's blanket ban on handgun possession inside a person's home violates the Second Amendment, as does its prohibition against rendering any lawful firearm in the home operable for the purpose of immediate self-defense. The opinion added, "Assuming that Heller is not disqualified from the exercise of Second Amendment rights, the District must permit him to register his handgun and must issue him a license to carry it in the home." Note that the *Heller* Court did not rule on the constitutionality of carrying weapons outside the home.

Heller stands for the principle that the right to bear arms belongs to individuals, not just to militias. However, *Heller* only applied to gun laws in federally-controlled jurisdictions, such as the District of Columbia. *Heller* did not address the application of the Second Amendment to state and local gun regulations.

Justice John Paul Stevens wrote one of two dissenting opinions in *Heller*. According to Justice Stevens, *Miller* held that the Second Amendment protects the right to keep and bear arms for military purposes, but does not curtail the legislature's power to regulate the nonmilitary use and ownership of weapons. Justice Scalia's opinion disputes that interpretation of *Miller*.

3. *McDonald v. City of Chicago*, 130 S.Ct. 3020 (2010.) Like *Heller*, *McDonald* was a 5-4 decision. The majority held that the Due Process Clause of the Fourteenth Amendment incorporates the Second Amendment right recognized in *Heller*; thus, individuals throughout the United States have the right to possess handguns in their homes for the purpose of self-defense.

Justice Antonin Scalia wrote, in a concurring opinion, that while he did not agree that the Fourteenth Amendment should be construed as incorporating the

Bill of Rights, he was resigned to that policy due to U.S. Supreme Court precedents.

Justice Clarence Thomas wrote a separate opinion, concurring in the result, but disagreeing with the plurality's reliance on the Due Process Clause as the basis for applying the Second Amendment to the states. He argued that individuals have the right to bear arms on account of the Fourteenth Amendment's Privileges and Immunities Clause.

Justices John Paul Stevens, Stephen Breyer, Ruth Bader Ginsburg and Sonia Sotomayor dissented from the majority's opinion in *McDonald*.

The Court's interpretation of the scope of the Second Amendment right has continued to evolve since the *McDonald* decision. In 2013, Highland Park, Illinois, a suburb of Chicago, passed an ordinance prohibiting the possession, sale, or manufacture of assault weapons. The ordinance was intended to address the potential threat of mass shootings involving semi-automatic weapons. An Illinois man, with the help of the Illinois State Rifle Association, challenged the law in federal court, arguing that the ban violated the man's constitutional rights. The federal trial and appeals courts upheld the ordinance, and plaintiff appealed to the U.S. Supreme Court. In 2015, on the heels of the tragic massacre of fourteen workers at a San Bernadino, California facility for people with developmental disabilities by two individuals wielding semi-automatic assault rifles, the Court declined to review the decision of the lower courts. Hence, the law banning private possession of assault weapons has been allowed to stand. (See *Friedman v. City of Highland Park, Illinois*, 577 U.S. ___ (2015).)

4. *United States v. Castleman*, 134 S.Ct. 1405 (2014). All nine Justices agreed that Castleman should be convicted under the federal Gun Control Act. The Act makes it unlawful for any person who has been convicted in any court for a misdemeanor crime of

domestic violence to transport or possess any firearms that have been affected by interstate commerce.

The central issue addressed was whether Castleman's Tennessee conviction for the misdemeanor offense of having "intentionally or knowingly caused bodily injury to the mother of his child" qualifies as a misdemeanor crime of domestic violence under the Act. The case holds that it does.

Counsel for Castleman also argued that the federal statute should be read narrowly because it implicates his Second Amendment right to keep and bear arms. The Court summarily dismissed that argument. As the High Court pointed out in *Heller*, Second Amendment rights are not unlimited.

Two years after deciding *Castleman*, the Supreme Court addressed the question of whether a "reckless assault" qualifies as a "use of force" under the federal Gun Control Act, which bans misdemeanor domestic violence offenders from possessing a gun for the rest of their lives. The case, *Voisine v. United States*, 579 U.S. ___ (2016), involved two men, each of whom had been previously convicted of violating a Maine statute that made it a misdemeanor to "intentionally, knowingly or recklessly cause bodily injury or offensive physical conduct to another person." Voisine had pleaded guilty to assaulting his girlfriend in violation of that Maine statute. Voisine objected to his conviction for violating the federal Gun Control Act because his prior conviction could have been based on reckless, rather than knowing or intentional conduct. The Court, in a 6-2 decision, held that a misdemeanor conviction for "recklessly" assaulting a domestic relation does disqualify an individual from ever possessing a gun, pursuant to federal law. Justice Elena Kagan delivered the opinion of the Court.

5. *Heller* explicitly approved of "laws imposing conditions and qualifications on the commercial sale of arms." However, in *Abramski v. United States*, 134 S.Ct.

2259 (2014), only a narrow 5-4 majority of the Justices voted to enforce the criminal penalty contained in the federal Gun Control Act against a straw purchaser who buys a gun for a person who is eligible to purchase it on his own. Abramski was a former police officer who bought a Glock 19 handgun for his uncle, who paid Abramski $400 for the gun. *Abramski* holds that a straw purchaser of a gun is subject to criminal penalties under the federal Gun Control Act for lying about the identity of the purchaser, regardless of the purchaser's eligibility.

It did not matter that the uncle met the legal requirements to purchase a gun, the Court said, because lying about the identity of the purchaser would defeat one of the main purposes of the Act -- enabling police to solve crimes by tracing the ownership of weapons later used in committing crimes.

VI. Crime And Punishment

1. *Duncan v. Louisiana*, 391 U.S. 145 (1968). In a 7-2 decision, the High Court concluded that a jury trial is a fundamental right, essential for preventing miscarriage of justice. Accordingly, the Court held that the Fourteenth Amendment guarantees a right to a jury trial in all criminal cases which, were they to be tried in a federal court, would come within the Sixth Amendment's guarantee.

The Court ruled that Duncan was entitled to a jury trial because he was charged with an offense carrying a sentence of up to two years of incarceration. The mere fact that Duncan was only sentenced to 60 days in the parish prison did not persuade the Court that simple battery should be deemed a "petty offense" for which a jury trial would not be required under the Sixth Amendment. The penalty authorized for a particular crime is of major relevance in determining whether it is a serious crime, the Court said.

2. In a 1972 case, *Furman v. Georgia*, 408 U.S. 238, the United States Supreme Court considered the constitutionality of Georgia's death penalty statute. By a vote of 5-4, the Court effectively struck down the death penalty laws of Georgia and 38 other states, and prohibited states from executing about 600 persons then on death row by holding that imposing the death penalty under existing standardless laws constituted cruel and unusual punishment.

Justice Thurgood Marshall, in a concurring opinion, took note of studies showing that capital punishment was imposed discriminatorily against certain identifiable classes of people. For example, he observed, "Negroes were executed far more often than whites in proportion to their percentage of the population."

3. *Gregg v. Georgia*, 428 U.S. 153 (1976). Following the decision in *Furman*, 35 states revised their death penalty statutes. *Gregg v. Georgia* reconsidered the constitutionality of Georgia's death penalty statute after Georgia legislators passed a new law providing detailed procedures, including a "bifurcated" trial whereby the question of guilt is decided in stage one, and the penalty is decided in stage two. Georgia's revised statute required that the jury find at least one of ten "aggravating" circumstances had been proved beyond a reasonable doubt in order to impose the death penalty.

In a 7-2 decision, the *Gregg* court decided that the death penalty did not violate the Constitution *per se*. The Court found that Georgia had cured the Constitutional defects inherent in its previous sentencing law, since it provided a set of standards to be met before a jury could hand down a death sentence.

4. *Apprendi v. New Jersey*, 530 U.S. 466 (2000). A narrow majority of the Justices held that, other than the fact of a prior conviction, any fact that increases the penalty for a crime beyond the prescribed statutory maximum must be submitted to a jury, and proved

beyond a reasonable doubt. The practice of allowing a judge to determine, by a preponderance of the evidence, a fact that constitutes an element of a crime, violates the defendant's Sixth Amendment right to a trial by jury and the Due Process Clause of the Fourteenth Amendment.

5. *Alleyne v. United States*, 133 S.Ct. 2151 (2013). In a 5-4 decision, the United States Supreme Court held that any fact that increases the mandatory minimum penalty for an offense constitutes an "element" of the offense, and therefore must be submitted to a jury. The jury must then determine whether this fact has been proved beyond a reasonable doubt. Where the trial judge substitutes his or her own judgment for the jury's determination regarding a factual matter affecting sentencing, the trial judge thereby violates the defendant's Sixth Amendment right to a jury trial.

The Court's decision in *Alleyne* is consistent with both the *Apprendi* decision described above and *Ring v. Arizona*, 536 U.S. 584 (2002). *Ring* held that those being tried in a capital case, like non-capital defendants, are entitled to have a jury decide any fact that could result in an increase in their maximum punishment.

Justice Antonin Scalia, concurring in *Ring*, emphasized that, "the fundamental meaning of the jury-trial guarantee of the Sixth Amendment is that all facts essential to the imposition of the level of punishment that the defendant receives ... must be found by the jury beyond a reasonable doubt."

At the time *Alleyne* was decided, the laws in three states, Alabama, Delaware, and Florida, still allowed trial judges to override jury verdicts of life without parole in capital punishment cases. Then in 2016, the High Court held in *Hurst v. Florida*, 577 U.S. ___ (2016), that Florida's sentencing scheme violated the Sixth Amendment because Florida employed a "hybrid" proceeding in which a jury renders an advisory verdict, but the judge makes the ultimate sentencing determinations. In order for the sentencing scheme to pass constitutional muster in a death penalty case, the jury must make factual findings regarding the existence of mitigating or aggravating factors, the Court said.

6. *Burrage v. United States*, 134 S.Ct. 881 (2014). In a unanimous decision, the High Court held that, at least where use of the drug distributed by the defendant is not an independently sufficient cause of the victim's death or serious bodily injury, a defendant cannot be liable under the penalty enhancement provisions of the drug law unless such use is a "but-for" cause of the death or injury.

7. *Alvin Ford v. Wainwright*, 477 U.S. 399 (1986). While incarcerated for a murder committed in the 1970s, Ford's mental state regressed to the point where he became incoherent. A psychiatrist concluded in 1983 that Ford suffered from a severe, uncontrollable mental disease that closely resembled paranoid schizophrenia. A second doctor met with Ford, and concluded that there was no reasonable possibility that Ford was dissembling or malingering.

In accordance with a Florida statute, Florida's Governor appointed a panel of three psychiatrists to evaluate whether Ford had the mental capacity to understand the nature of the death penalty and why it was being imposed on him. Neither Ford nor his lawyer was allowed to participate in the 30-minute interview by the three doctors, who determined that, while Ford may have been psychotic, he did understand what was going to happen to him.

The High Court narrowed the issue in the case to whether the Eighth Amendment prohibits the execution of the insane. In a 7-2 decision, the Court held that, since the Eighth Amendment applies to defendants tried in state as well as federal courts, the Amendment prohibits a state from carrying out a sentence of death upon a prisoner who is insane.

8. *Atkins v. Virginia*, 536 U.S. 304 (2002). In a 6-3 decision, the Court held that executions of mentally retarded criminals constitute "cruel and unusual punishment" prohibited by the Eighth Amendment. The then Chief Justice, William Rehnquist, filed a dissenting opinion, in which Justices Antonin Scalia and Clarence Thomas joined.

    The Court had dodged the question of whether the death penalty should ever be imposed on a mentally retarded criminal in *Penry v. Lynaugh*, 492 U.S. 302 (1989). In *Penry*, the Court opted to leave that determination to state legislatures. Thirteen years after *Penry*, the *Atkins* court found that the time had come to pronounce that the practice was barred by the Eighth Amendment because state after state had consistently adopted death penalty laws exempting the mentally retarded.

9. *Roper v. Simmons*, 543 U.S. 551 (2005). In a 5-4 decision, the High Court held that the Eighth Amendment forbids execution of offenders who are under the age of eighteen when they commit a crime.

    The Court found that the two societal goals underlying capital punishment -- deterrence and retribution -- are not served by executing juveniles because juveniles do not engage in the kind of cost-benefit analysis that adults do. Moreover, due to their youth and immaturity, their conduct is less morally reprehensible than that of adults. The factor that cinched the Court's decision was evidence of a broad national consensus among U.S. states that those under eighteen should not be executed. The opinion in *Roper* emphasizes the parallels between this case and *Atkins*.

    The mantra that the Eighth Amendment "must draw its meaning from the evolving standards of decency that mark the progress of a maturing society" comes from a 1958 case, *Trop v. Dulles*, 356 U.S. 86.

Five years after the *Roper v. Simmons* decision, the Court held, in *Graham v. Florida*, 560 U.S. 48 (2010), that the Eighth Amendment's Cruel and Unusual Punishments Clause does not permit a juvenile offender to be sentenced to life in prison without parole for a non-homicide crime.

In 2012, the Court went one step further by holding, in *Miller v. Alabama*, 132 S.Ct. 2455 (2012), that a mandatory life sentence without parole for those under the age of eighteen at the time of their crimes violates the Eighth Amendment, even where the crime is a homicide. Miller was a 14-year-old who simply went along with older boys to rob a video store, but may not have been aware of their intent to use lethal force, and did not participate in the homicide of the store's clerk.

Then in 2016, the Court took up the question of whether *Miller* applies retroactively to juveniles whose convictions and sentences were final when *Miller* was decided. *Montgomery v. Louisiana*, 577 U.S. ___ (2016), answers the question in the affirmative. It holds that all those who were convicted long ago as juveniles must be considered for parole or given a new sentence.

10. *Hall v. Florida*, 134 S.Ct. 1986 (2014). Justice Anthony Kennedy penned the opinion on behalf of a 5-4 majority, which held that Florida's rule of thumb for executing mentally retarded convicts was unconstitutional. The rule exempted mentally retarded convicts from execution only if their I.Q. score was 70 or less. The Court said such a rigid rule creates an unacceptable risk that persons with intellectual disability will be executed, thereby violating the Eighth Amendment. The Court deemed the practice to be "cruel and unusual" because only a small and diminishing number of states continue to employ a fixed I.Q. cutoff. Most of the states that emphasize I.Q. scores tend to apply a standard error of measurement with a range of numbers, so that an I.Q. of 70 is represented by a band of 65 to 75. Clinicians take into account additional

factors, such as the person's inability to adapt to his social and cultural environment, behavioral records, school tests and reports, and testimony regarding past behavior.

TABLE OF CASES
(References are to pages)

Abramski; United States v., 180
Aguilar v. Texas, 60, n.22
Alleyne v. United States, 188
Apprendi v. New Jersey, 186
Argersinger v. Hamlin, 159
Arizona v. Gant, 37
Arizona v. Lemon Johnson, 94
Atkins v. Virginia, 195
Atwater v. City of Lago Vista, 124
Bailey v. United States, 96
Berghuis v. Thompkins, 150
Betts v. Brady, 140, n.2
Birchfield v. North Dakota, 46
Bivens v. Six Unknown Federal Narcotics Agents, 106
Brendlin v. California, 92
Brinegar v. United States, 23, n.5
Brown v. Texas, 50
Burrage v. United States, 191
Burt v. Titlow, 167
California v. Ciraolo, 74, n. 27
Camara v. Municipal Court, 103
Cantwell v. Connecticut, 3
Castleman; United States v., 178
Chaplinsky v. New Hampshire, 5
Chimel v. California, 33
Cox v. Louisiana, 11, n.5
Delaware v. Prouse, 30
Dickerson v. United States, 147, n.8
District of Columbia v. Heller, 172
Duncan v. Louisiana, 182
Edwards v. South Carolina, 11
Escobedo v. Illinois, 143
Fernandez v. California, 100
Florence v. County of Burlington, 133
Florida v. Bostick, 55
Florida v. Jardines, 72

Florida v. Riley, 74, n. 27
Florida v. Royer, 53, n.18
Ford v. Wainwright, 193
Friedman v. Highland Park, 176, n.3
Furman v. Georgia, 184
Georgia v. Randolph, 98
Gideon v. Wainwright, 140
Graham v. Connor, 114
Graham v. Florida, 197, n.9
Gregg v. Georgia, 184
Griffin v. California, 146
Hall v. Florida, 198
Heien v. North Carolina, 30, n.7
Herring v. United States, 69
Hiibel v. Nevada, 51
Houston, Texas v. Hill, 9
Hurst v. Florida, 188, n.5
Illinois v. Caballes, 81
Illinois v. Gates, 60
Indianapolis v. Edmond, 59
J.D.B. v. North Carolina, 157
Johnson v. Zerbst, 140, n.1
Jones; United States v., 76
Katz v. United States, 21
Kyllo v. United States, 74, n.28
Lafler v. Cooper, 164
Leon; United States v., 66
Lewis v. New Orleans, 7
Malley v. Briggs, 108
Malloy v. Hogan, 146, n.7
Mapp v. Ohio, 17
Maryland v. King, 43
Maryland v. Wilson, 90
McDonald v. City of Chicago, 176
Mendenhall; United States v., 53
Messerschmidt v. Millender, 136
Michigan v. Sitz, 57
Michigan v. Summers, 96, n.40
Miller v. Alabama, 197, n.9

Miller v. United States, 172, n.1
Minnesota v. Olson, 15
Miranda v. Arizona, 147
Missouri v. Frye, 164
Missouri v. McNeely, 40
Monell v. Department of Social Services, 107
Monroe v. Pape, 107, n.2
Montgomery v. Louisiana, 197, n.9
Mullenix v. Luna, 118, n.8
Navarette v. California, 27
Neil v. Biggers, 169
New York v. Quarles, 147, n.8
Olmstead v. United States, 21, n.4
Ontario v. Quon, 127
Payton v. New York, 14
Pearson v. Callahan, 110
Pennsylvania v. Mimms, 49
Penry v. Lynaugh, 195, n.8
Perry v. New Hampshire, 169, n.18
Plumhoff v. Rickard, 118
Rakas v. Illinois, 88
Riley v. California, 79
Ring v. Arizona, 188, n.5
Robinson; United States v., 35
Rodriguez v. United States, 83
Roper v. Simmons, 197
Ryburn v. Huff, 121
Safford v. Redding, 131
Salinas v. Texas, 153
Schmerber v. California, 40, n.12
Schneckloth v. Bustamonte, 85
Scott v. Harris, 118, n.8
See v. City of Seattle, 103, n.43
Spinelli v. United States, 60, n.22
Strickland v. Washington, 161
Tennessee v. Garner, 112
Terry v. Ohio, 23
Tolan v. Cotton, 116
Trop v. Dulles, 197, n.9

United States v. (see name of defendant)
Utah v. Strieff, 66, n.24
Voisine v. United States, 178, n.4
Welsh v. Wisconsin, 14, n.1
Whren v. United States, 32
Wolf v. Colorado, 17, n.3
Wong Sun v. United States, 63
Wurie; United States v., 79

About the Author

The author earned B.A. and J.D. degrees at the University of Chicago. She directed the National Study Commission on Defense Services, which developed national standards for public defender and appointed counsel systems. She also served as a public defender and private criminal defense lawyer, and as an Assistant Illinois Attorney General, handling appeals. As an adjunct professor, she taught a variety of law school and college classes on criminal justice.

As a prelude to writing this book, she wrote a monthly subscription publication for law enforcement officers, designed to inform police about evolving court mandates governing police-citizen interactions and the individual rights of citizens.

Her published work includes numerous articles on criminal justice and three books: *Guide to Establishing a Defender System*; *Insider's Guide to Divorce in Illinois*; and a biography, *A Cubed and His Algebra*.

Made in the USA
San Bernardino, CA
16 March 2017